P9-DBO-692

7-20-74

Behold His Love

Page 80

Behold His Love

Basilea Schlink

DIMENSION BOOKS
BETHANY FELLOWSHIP, INC.
Minneapolis, Minnesota

Originally published in England by Marshall, Morgan, & Scott, Ltd., London.

First British Edition, 1973
First American Edition, 1974

Unless otherwise stated, all Bible quotations are taken from the Revised Standard Version of the Bible, copyrighted 1946 and 1952 by the Division of Christian Education of the National Council of the Churches of Christ in the U.S.A., and used by permission.

ISBN 0-87123-039-9

DIMENSION BOOKS
are published by Bethany Fellowship, Inc.
6820 Auto Club Road, Minneapolis, Minnesota

Printed in the United States of America

CONTENTS

O that I could keep mourning,
Yes, mourning ceaselessly,
Lamenting Jesus' suffering,
That all might come to see:
He longs to have us near Him,
But we reject His way,
His cross we are not sharing,
Avoid it day by day.

 If we really behold the suffering of Jesus, it will make a deep impression upon our life. Nothing but His amazing love could have compelled Him to suffer for us in the way in which He did. Nothing can bring us closer to Jesus than meditating upon His passion. Therefore, if we wish to come closer to the heart of Jesus, we should immerse ourselves in His suffering all the year and not only during Lent.

Meditation upon the passion of Jesus can bring us to repentance and awaken a deep love for Him in our hearts. Surely nothing can help us to see our sin more clearly than to behold the suffering that Jesus endured to save us from sin. Countless people, who have suddenly seen what Jesus endured for their sake, have broken down in tears of repentance and adoration of the Lamb of God. This mighty power lies hidden in the suffering of Jesus. But that is not all. Those who come to true repentance long to follow in Jesus' footsteps. Their ardent love for Him compels them to do so. Those who have wept over their sins, in view of Jesus' bitter suffering for their sake, respond to Him with all their heart. Full of gratitude, they are therefore sensitive to His call, "Come, take up your cross and follow Me". So it was long ago, and still is today, for Jesus Christ is the same yesterday, today and forever.

Still He goes from land to land, revealing Himself in His suffering, seeking to draw our hearts to Him, so that we can see Him today being tried, scourged, crowned with thorns and carrying the cross. But this is not all. When Jesus reveals

Himself to us in His suffering, He is seeking disciples, just as He did long ago. Now that He, the Head, is in heaven, He longs for the members of His Body to represent Him on earth. This means that they must follow His way of the cross. His followers will also say, "Yes Father", when they are tempted. They will silently endure reproaches and accusations. They will willingly accept being scorned and despised. They will humbly bear the burden of a cross.

Yes, Jesus goes from land to land, from church to church. To each one who confesses His name He says: "I have trodden the path of suffering. Will you follow Me and take up your cross, that others may see My image in you? I long for the world to see that I am eternal Love. I emptied Myself, becoming poor, lowly and despised. I was sorely wounded in body and soul and gave Myself as a sacrifice for you, all out of love for you."

The world needs signposts. It does not want merely to hear sermons. Indeed many people have heard too many sermons. The world needs something that can be seen. It needs to see people who live like Jesus, the Lamb, who are triumphant in suffering. It needs to see people who humbly bear their crosses yet show love and mercy towards those responsible for their suffering. It needs to see people who endure every burden but still continue to trust in Jesus' victory—for their own lives as well as for others.

The world would take notice, if it saw people who endured being despised, slandered and persecuted without retaliating. If these people not only bore everything, but even blessed their enemies and those who wronged them, it would indeed make an impact upon the world.

An invisible stream of love would flow forth into this hate-saturated world. This power of love would gradually destroy the forces of hatred. Jesus' passion shows us that love alone is stronger than hatred. Love that suffers and bears all things must become visible on earth. The world is waiting for Jesus' love to be manifested among His people. Heaven is also waiting, for the Body of Jesus Christ must unite in the same Spirit as its Head, if it is to show forth His life.

The world will take notice when it sees people who lovingly accept God's will, no matter where it leads them; people who bind themselves to God and humbly allow themselves to be led by His powerful hand. Others will suddenly see Jesus in them—Jesus, taken prisoner and led to trial. The world will take notice when it sees people who trust Jesus to solve all their problems, and who patiently bear their burdens of sickness, loneliness, difficult family circumstances or other troubles. They bend low beneath the weight of their cross. They do not rebel, because they recognize themselves as sinners who need and deserve God's discipline and chastening. Such people are radiant and powerful. From them, there pour forth streams of living water. Through them, Jesus becomes visible, and the world will see and believe the Gospel.

Not only the world waits for this to happen. Jesus waits too. His eyes look down upon each land, desiring to find someone who walks the way He walked, and who reflects His image. Only people such as these can help Him to build the Kingdom of God. His kingdom will not come through service alone—no matter how necessary that may be. He Himself established it through suffering. Therefore, until the end of the world, it will be built only by those who are willing to suffer with Jesus and, like grains of wheat, be buried in the ground.

Jesus' passion poses this question for us: Who are truly Jesus' disciples? Only those who take up their cross and follow Him. This is where true disciples are divided from nominal Christians. Our attitude to the passion reveals our true attitude towards Jesus. The disciple who is willing to bear the cross, to accept lowliness, disgrace, accusations and false reproaches, proves that He loves Jesus and takes His call seriously.

How God must weep, when He finds so few who are willing to follow Him and bear their cross! When we meditate upon the various stations of the cross, Jesus does not want us merely to lament His suffering and worship Him in adoration. Of course, we are called to do this. But He also wants us to be captivated by His suffering. Then, out of love and gratitude, we shall be set on fire to follow Him, and will depict a little of His suffering in our lives.

Power lies in what is lived and practised—there is more power in actions than in words. Speeches are easily made, but deeds are powerful when they spring out of a love which is compelled to sacrifice and suffer.

More is accomplished for the Kingdom of God by the person who follows God along difficult paths, in patience, humility and love, than by the eloquent preacher who does not live a life of unconditional discipleship. For it is only life that gives birth to life. A grain of wheat must fall into the ground and die. In the same way, our ego must be crucified daily, if new life is to be brought forth. Jesus promises that those who go the way of the cross will bear much fruit.

So Jesus' passion poses a personal question to each one of us: Do we walk in His way day by day? Does the Father see in us the traits of His Son? He longs for those He created in His image to resemble Him. Are we sharing His way so that we can become like Him?

Jesus' passion calls for cross-bearers. It is these who will form the true Church, for there will be no dissension or division between them. They will be like the Lamb, who neither reviled, nor demanded His rights, but endured and loved. The world will see that they are Jesus' disciples, because they love one another and are united in love. True cross-bearers are one in spirit, even though they may belong to different denominations and may not even know each other. But whenever they meet, they recognize each other by the sign of bearing the cross. The same love for Jesus, the Lamb of God, brings them closely together around Him.

This book is addressed to those who would like to meditate prayerfully on Jesus' passion, so that repentance might continually be awakened in them. Then love and gratitude to Jesus, the Man of Sorrows, will lead them more and more into the way of the cross and into unity of love with those who love Him.

My Lord Jesus,

I implore You, let me not be a Christian in name only nor a mere spectator of Your passion, but rather Your cross-bearer, following in Your footsteps. As a true member of Your Body, let my life reflect Your image.

I place myself in Your hands so that You can imprint upon me the traits of the Lamb. Help me to endure willingly all that people do to me. May I remain silent when I am unjustly accused. Teach me to bless those who curse me and those who hate and persecute me. I will humble myself beneath scorn and disgrace and patiently bear every cross that comes to me. I know they come from Your hands. People are just Your instruments.

I thank You that I can rely on the words of Scripture and need no longer live for myself alone, but may let Christ live in me. You are the Lamb of God, who endured all things in love. Come into my heart anew as I meditate upon Your passion, and imprint in me Your humility and love. As I use these meditations, help me to thank You for the suffering that You endured because of my sin. Help me to show You my love and gratitude, not merely in words, but also in deeds.

GETHSEMANE

And he came out, and went, as was his custom, to the Mount
of Olives; and the disciples followed him. And when he came
to the place he said to them, "Pray that you may not enter
into temptation." And he withdrew from them about a
stone's throw, and knelt down and prayed, "Father, if thou
art willing, remove this cup from me; nevertheless not my
will, but thine, be done." And there appeared to him an angel
from heaven, strengthening him. And being in an agony he
prayed more earnestly; and his sweat became like great
drops of blood falling down upon the ground. And when he
rose from prayer, he came to the disciples and found them
sleeping for sorrow, and he said to them, "Why do you
sleep? Rise and pray that you may not enter into temptation."

Luke 22: 39–46

Gethsemane—
who hears His pleading,
His fearful crying and entreating?
The Son of God in anguished fear
With none to solace Him is here.
He is alone, forsaken.

Gethsemane—
who notes His yearning,
Who sees Him to His friends now turning,
That He may all His grief impart,
And they may cheer, console His heart?
Alas! His friends are sleeping.

15

Gethsemane—
who sees Him wrestling,
With evil powers around Him pressing,
Tormenting Him with all their might?
And in His soul He sees no light,
By God and man forsaken!

W.J.53*

* W.J. indicates songs taken from *Well-Spring of Joy*

OBEDIENCE — THE STURDY STAFF

Scripture reading: Matthew 26:36–41

Although he was a Son, he learned obedience
through what he suffered; and being made
perfect he became the source of eternal salvation to all who obey him.

Hebrews 5:8, 9

The dread darkness of evil forces surrounded Jesus in Gethsemane. He must have almost died in the midst of such
raging of hell. How He must have longed for a staff to lean
upon during this hour of temptation. Hell was trying to
devour him. But there was no staff. His disciples, who should
have supported Him, proved useless. But God showed Jesus a
different staff, which brought Him safely through the night
of temptation: blind obedience. Jesus used this staff of obedience to the will of the Father to bring Him through that
dreadful hour. It brought Him victory in that mighty battle,
when He stood alone, facing the combined forces of hell.

Now, whenever we are in temptation, Jesus offers us this
same staff. It enables us to find the right way in the dark. It
leads us to victory in the struggle against temptation. This
staff of obedience to the Word of God and His com-
mandments also involves obeying the admonitions, exhor-
tations, commands and promises which we receive as
personal words of guidance. The man who walks step by
step in the way God has shown him, without looking to the
right or left, will never be conquered by the enemy.

The greater and more blessed our ministry is to be, the
greater the temptations we will have to endure. For when
Satan sees that a human life is accomplishing great things
for the Kingdom of God, he goes into battle. God permits
him to do so, in order that His disciples' obedience may be

tested and proved. If the disciples overcome, their lives will receive a double endowment of power. They will become pillars in His kingdom and one day they will receive the crown of life.

Jesus led the way as the "pioneer of our salvation". Now, if we follow Him, our way will also end in victory.

Such anguished grief and pain You felt,
As by the garden rock You knelt;
For comfort You must seek in vain,
That sinners grace and mercy gain,
* O Comforter divine.*

Lord Jesus,

I thank You that You endured being bitterly tempted by the enemy in Gethsemane. Because of this, I know that You understand my temptations. I thank You for standing beside me in times of temptation, as my Brother and Helper. You will not hand me over to Satan. I thank You for the assurance that You could do no such thing, for You fought the battle in Gethsemane for our sake, for my sake, so that the enemy should no longer have any right to me. How can any temptation be mightier than You? In Gethsemane You totally defeated Satan and his temptations. I believe in Your victory in Gethsemane and call upon Your name, Jesus. You have power over my temptations. The enemy will yield!

VICTORY THROUGH HUMBLE SUBMISSION

Scripture reading: Mark 14:32–46

During his life on earth, Jesus offered up prayer and entreaty, aloud and in silent tears, to the one who had the power to save him out of death, and he submitted so humbly that his prayer was heard.

Hebrews 5:7 (Jerusalem Bible)

We know that Jesus was "greatly distressed and troubled" during the battle of Gethsemane. Whoever won this victory would win mankind! Everything looked as though Satan and his kingdom would win. Yet Jesus had a weapon which proved to be a mighty weapon and brought Him victory: humble submission.

In paradise Adam and Eve fell in the hour of temptation. They lost their battle with Satan because they sought their own glory. The serpent said to them: "You will be like God if you do what I tell you." Because we desire to be important and have power and glory like God, we also give in to temptation.

Jesus was the only one who did not seek His own glory, but the glory of the Father. He proved this through humble submission and obedience to the Father's will. Through this obedience He glorified God. "Father, Your will is perfect." So "his prayer was heard", that is, He was victorious.

Now Jesus has given us a weapon to overcome every temptation: humble submission to the will of God and to His chastenings. This glorifies God and the enemy will not gain control of our soul.

My Lord Jesus,

I will listen no longer to the enemy's voice. I will listen to You, the Good Shepherd. In Gethsemane You wrestled alone

19

with the powers of death—for my sake, because You love me. You will lead me in the best way. I will trust You, even if the way is painful and hard. You, the Good Shepherd, cannot lead me in false paths. Your love could not do this. I trust You to recall me when I go astray. You will not let me fall into the hands of the enemy. I am so precious to You that, for my sake, You fought the battle against Satan in Gethsemane.

So I thank You for the knowledge that during my battles and temptations I am in Your hands, the hands of eternal love. I want to trust in Your love and follow You step by step in obedience to Your words and Your guidance.

JESUS, ALONE AGAINST THE HOSTS OF HELL

Scripture reading: Luke 22:44-46

Insults have broken my heart, so that I am in despair. I looked for pity, but there was none, and for comforters, but I found none.
Psalm 69:20

Jesus was victorious in Gethsemane. But what did it cost Him? We know that He wrestled with death—that is, with Satan, the prince of death. It was a battle between life and death so that "His sweat became like great drops of blood falling down upon the ground" (Luke 22:44). Those hellish spirits squeezed blood out of Him as they endeavoured to torment Him to death. How unimaginable and dreadful must their raging have been!

In this battle with hell Jesus' soul was tormented. We know that temptations can make us sick in body, soul and spirit. Not just a few spirits of hell came to attack Jesus, but probably every one. All the forces of hell came to make an all-out attack against the Lord of the kingdom of light. Jesus stood all alone. He had no one to aid Him. Yet He could have had a thousand times ten thousand standing at His side, to fight against these forces of evil. But of all these thousands of angels, only one came to bring Him a strengthening drink.

How greatly Jesus must have suffered under the pressure of the powers of hell! He would not otherwise have fled from these devilish hosts three times, to go to His disciples. Scarcely could He comprehend how they could sleep while all hell was raging to destroy their Master and His work. How the powers of hell must have tormented Him, that He should have sought help from a poor bunch of sinners and humbly asked them to stand at His side! The fact that His plea remained unanswered by His disciples in this hour of dreadful torment stands as an eternal indictment against us and all Christians. For we too have deserted Jesus in His deepest suffering.

Today, as great High Priest, He still wrestles to draw human souls from the clutches of hell. He still calls us to stand with Him. If we are not engaged with Him in saving lost souls, we are once more deserting Him.

He who loves everyone as no other ever could, was left alone by His own in the hour of need. Today He is still alone, as He continues to struggle for the souls of men. He is seeking co-workers, co-sufferers, co-sacrificers for His work. But who hears His heart-rending plea?

I hear a voice lamenting
Through all the world today.
O who can be tormenting
God's Son again this way?
Gethsemane repeating,
He suffers once again.
The world the Lamb is leaving
Alone in grief and pain.

Men want His love and healing,
But will not go His way.
His grief He is revealing,
But none with Him will stay.
As once men slept and left You
In agony alone,
We still today continue
To leave You on Your own.

Lord Jesus,

I humble myself, because I am no different from Your disciples. I let You stand alone and am not with You, praying and wrestling for human souls. I am deeply sorry that You must continue lamenting about Your own, "Could you not watch with me for one hour?" Often I have failed to listen to Your quiet bidding to come to You in prayer. My work and other things have seemed to be more important to me than You. Sometimes I have given in to sleep rather than answer Your request.

Forgive me for making You wait, because You were worth less to me than my work and my sleep. I show so little respect and love for You. Accept my dedication today and let me follow the admonitions of Your Spirit and come to You in prayer. May my best time be set aside for You, Lord Jesus, to be spent in prayer.

"IN VAIN"?

Scripture reading: Luke 22:41–46

But I said, "I have laboured in vain, I have spent my strength for nothing and vanity; yet surely my right is with the Lord, and my recompense with my God."

Isaiah 49:

What did Satan use to torment Jesus in the battle in Gethsemane? Satan was the accuser, so he must have ap proached Jesus with the most severe accusations. We can only guess how demoralizing and agonizing they were for Jesus. Perhaps the enemy told Jesus that His whole work of salvation would be in vain, because Christians themselves still would not change. Perhaps he demonstrated to Jesus how unredeemed Christians would be—unloving, irreconcilable, critical, untruthful and proud. They would plainly resemble those who do not believe in Him. Perhaps he reminded Jesus scornfully of His parting words to His disciples. In the farewell discourses, Jesus had said that the world would know His disciples by their love for one another. Yet they would instead become known for their dissension. Perhaps Satan showed Him how divided His Church would become later—into many different denominations and groups. Possibly he taunted Him, saying, "In vain! Your way is in vain! There will not be one solitary soul that You will truly have redeemed." Jesus' soul was so tormented and wounded by these accusations of the enemy that finally He cried out: "My Father, if it be possible, let this cup pass from me."

We can have no idea of the countless arguments which the enemy must have brought against Jesus. Probably the division and lack of love between Christians were not the only things for which Satan would have blamed Him. No, he is the supreme liar. He criticized God to Adam and Eve. He must also have blamed Jesus for all the evil things that man has ever done, because He is the Creator of man. Albrecht Dürer portrayed Jesus, nearing the end of His agony in Gethsemane, lying stretched out on the ground. Perhaps this is an accurate portrayal of what occurred. At this time Jesus may have taken all the sins of the world upon Himself, in spirit.

What gave Jesus the strength to hold out against all these dreadful accusations—against the taunt, "In vain!"? Only the surrender of His will to the will of the Father. Time and again Jesus said, "Not my will, but thine, be done." He repeated it now, when He could no longer understand the will

23

of the Father—when His work seemed to be in vain. In this manner He was victorious in the dreadful temptations of Gethsemane. He has marked out for us the way to victory, when our sacrificial way appears to be "in vain" and when we are oppressed by false accusations. Victory comes from the humble submission of our wills to the will of God.

Jesus shows us that there is no need for us to know whether our ministry and sacrifice are meaningful. The reverse is true. Through His battle in Gethsemane He proved The mightier the fruit of our ministry, the more sacrificial the way will be and the less meaningful our path will appear. The greater our ministry, the more frequent the enemy's accusation that we are wrongfully committed by going this way. But if we follow Jesus without attending to the voice of the enemy and remain obedient to God until the end, we will bear much fruit.

" YES, FATHER "

Scripture reading: Matthew 26:42–46

Jesus said to them, "My food is to do the will of him who sent me, and to accomplish his work."

John 4:34

We may say that when Jesus spoke the words "Yes Father" in Gethsemane, He made His decision to accept the crucifixion. With the affirmation of Gethsemane, the die was cast to enter upon the way of the cross. Jesus' decision did not occur—as we might think—at the time of the crucifixion, but in Gethsemane. For us also, the decisive point comes during temptation, not afterwards, as we are often inclined to think. The hours of temptation are hours of decision, with far-reaching significance. Our passing the test can become the basis for a powerful ministry, so that we, like Jesus, can lay down our lives for our brothers and produce eternal fruit. From hours of temptation hidden strengths emerge after the temptation itself is overcome. That is why Scripture says, "Count it all joy, my brethren, when you meet various trials" (James 1:2). Jesus shows us the way to overcome temptation with the words He spoke when horror and dread threatened Him: "Yes Father!"

The enemy, too, must depart from us when we say "Yes" to God over and over again. Thus we are also saying "Yes" to our problem or suffering. This affirmation makes us one with Him and unity will make us strong. When we are at one with God, because our wills are surrendered to Him in love, the enemy is powerless. He fears this unity. When we are weighed down with troubles and the darkness seeks to overwhelm us, we should say to God, "Do with me whatever You will, for as long as You see the need." The enemy departs from people who say this during hours of temptation. He recognizes that we are so humbly submitted to the will of God, that his assault cannot succeed. So he will release us.

Lord Jesus,

Help me to submit completely to Your will as You did to the Father. No matter what way the Father led You, You said, "Yes," to Him. I desire to say, "Yes Father" today, as You did, although my heart is crying and rebelling against my cross. The Father's love sustained You and enabled You to conquer all Your enemies so that You may now sit at Your Father's right hand. Your Father is also my Father and He has only good things designed for me. He will support me in a wonderful way and convert my temptation and sorrow into glory. Together with You, my Lord Jesus, I trust in the

Father's love. Therefore I say, "Yes" wholeheartedly. "D
with me as You will. Your will is best."

My Lord Jesus,
   You surrendered Yourself to the Father and drank th
cup. I too want to do this today, in the belief that You wi
not forsake me. You will send an angel to strengthen me.

FATHER AND SON—WHO SUFFERED MORE?

Scripture reading: Luke 22:39–43

For God so loved the world that he gave h
only begotten son.

John 3:16 (A.V

Jesus Christ, the "eternal Life", is the Light and the Sun c
the whole universe. Where did He now find Himself? In th
regions of death, in the company of hell! But He did not g
there as Lord. He had been deprived of His power as th
Lord of light and life. Like Samson, He had lost His supe
natural strength. He emptied Himself for our sake. In th
state He entered the battle against hell! How could th
Father permit such a thing? He allowed His Child to drai
Himself of all power and glory and then sent Him into th
hellish fight!
   All the angels and heavenly beings may indeed have l
mented as they saw their Lord and Creator so pitiful an
weak. Their Lord was deprived of all His divine power an
delivered into the hands of the spirits of hell for the battle a
Gethsemane! So stern was the Father's love! He saw His So

rembling. Heaven and earth were at His disposal. He could ave given the sun and moon to illumine the night. He could ave sent hosts of angels to support His Son. How the father's heart must have been torn with compassion. Yet He lid not help. Father, Son and Holy Spirit had, in love, agreed o suffer for our sakes. They chose the suffering of the ross.

But now the Son cried out to the Father, "My Father, if it e possible, let this cup pass from me." This incomparable gony must have pierced the Father's heart. His Son was alling to Him for help. He is the Father of all fatherhood nd is pure love. He always longs to answer His children—yet He did not answer Jesus. Then a second time the oice of the Son was heard. A second cry for help traversed he air to the Father's heart, "My Father." His Child, amid he pangs of death, was crying out to Him. The bloody sweat roke out on His Son as He wrestled with death. But the father did not stretch out His hand. He refused to intervene o free His Child from the devil's clutches and the hand of leath. He sent just one angel to strengthen Him.

We cannot tell who suffered more. The Son cried to the father in the agony of His death. The Father had to watch His Son writhing within the grasp of death but do nothing to help Him. He could not, because it had been ordained that esus would suffer. It was for our sake alone that the Father nd the Son determined voluntarily to undergo this dreadful orment! Truly God loves us so much; we are so precious to lim, that the Father Himself delivered up His only Son to leath. He delivered Him up to Gethsemane's night of leath.

The Father sees His Son alone,
The Son who always shared His throne;
Hosts from hell around Him springing,
With countless lies, anguish bringing.

His heart was pierced by cry of pain;
With Him His Son must plead in vain:
"Will You take this cup away?
Yet not My will, but Yours alway!"

But silent must the Father be,
For He would set lost sinners free;
Therefore is the Son forsaken,
A path of pain He has taken.

We can measure a person's love for us by the amount of suffering he is willing to undergo for our sake. The Father's suffering was immeasurable. He had to see His Son suffer so terribly. The torment was so great that Jesus' sweat was like drops of blood. Unfathomable was His agony in Gethsemane. Surrounded by the raging powers of hell, He cried to the Father for help. Unfathomable is God's suffering. Unfathomable and never-ending is His love for us. He cannot do otherwise than extricate us from the deepest pits of hellish temptations. He endured the depths of hell in Gethsemane, for this very purpose.

THE ARREST

So Judas, procuring a band of soldiers and some officers from the chief priests and the Pharisees, went there with lanterns and torches and weapons. Then Jesus, knowing all that was to befall him, came forward and said to them, "Whom do you seek?" They answered him, "Jesus of Nazareth." Jesus said to them, "I am he." Judas, who betrayed him, was standing with them. When he said to them, "I am he," they drew back and fell to the ground. Again he asked them, "Whom do you seek?" And they said, "Jesus of Nazareth." Jesus answered, "I told you that I am he; so, if you seek me, let these men go." This was to fulfil the word which he had spoken, "Of those whom thou gavest me I lost not one." Then Simon Peter, having a sword, drew it and struck the high priest's slave and cut off his right ear. The slave's name was Malchus. Jesus said to Peter, "Put your sword into its sheath; shall I not drink the cup which the Father has given me?" So the band of soldiers and their captain and the officers of the Jews seized Jesus and bound him.

John 18:3–12

Jesus now shows to me,
Though bound, we can be free,
Christ pioneering the way.
All that His Father willed,
Jesus in love fulfilled,
To set us free from our chains.

Bound as a lamb He's led,
Crucified in our stead.
Watch how He goes to His death.
Lo, God in fetters see,
He waits for those who'll be
Willing to wear chains like Him.

W.J.57

UNMASKED !

Scripture reading: Luke 22:47–53

When I was with you day after day in the temple, you did not lay hands on me. But this is your hour, and the power of darkness.

Luke 22:53

In the hour of Jesus' arrest, masks were suddenly dropped and faces changed. It was like the climax of a drama in which the actors are unveiled and their true faces are instantly revealed. In a similar way, the masks fell when Jesus was arrested. Everyone present was suddenly unveiled and their wickedness and sin could clearly be seen.

How could one of the disciples become a traitor and all the others deserters? The Word of God has the answer: "This is your hour, and the power of darkness." For all of us there are times that we could call "our hour". These are decisive for our life and reveal what has been in us for a long time. It is often made plain in the Scriptures that everything depends upon a certain hour when we are tempted by inward or outward conditions. It is amazing what can emerge from a human heart in such an hour, if it has refused to listen to Jesus' admonitions. If we have neglected opportunities to repent of our sins, they will take a mighty revenge on us at these times.

Perhaps some people in the crowd were bitter, because Jesus had not helped them solve their problems. The elders and the Pharisees did not want Jesus to tell them the truth about themselves. How often we resemble them. Jesus had called them a "brood of vipers" and "white-washed tombs." Can we accept reproaches humbly without feeling the slightest bit hurt? Or do we feel bitterness or even hatred in our hearts? For us too an "hour of darkness" will come. God

31

wants to use the reproaches and accusations of others to judge and humble us. If we cannot accept them, bitterness and hatred will gather in our hearts. Then in the decisive hour, the "beast" in us that did not want to be judged and die, will rise up and rebel against Jesus.

For this reason Jesus had to suffer. He, the Light, had to expose Himself in the darkness so that we could see ourselves as we are. God leads us into such situations so that like Peter, we can be faced with our sin. Then we can repent. When we learn to weep for our sin, we can be forgiven and cleansed. In this manner we gain new strength. Later, like Peter, we shall be able to withstand the temptations of such hours.

Lord Jesus,

Let me look often at You as a prisoner. Let me see Your bound hands. Remould me in Your image as I gaze at You. I believe that there is a power in the picture of Your suffering that can make me become like You. O Lord, You allowed people, even Your enemies, to have their will with You. You still did good to them—You healed Malchus' ear. Help me to follow Your example. I believe that Your suffering and Your sacrificial death have saved me from all rebellion. You will prevent my rebelling against those who cross my will—even if they mistreat me. Yes, You have redeemed me to live a life of love—the love that suffers all things, endures all things and even blesses its enemies.

O Lamb in earthly chains,
Your link with God remains;
You ever press on to heaven,
Bringing with You all those
Who with You suffering chose
Joyfully to paradise.

So let us praise the Son,
Who dearly victory won,
Letting men bind Him so tight;
   Praise Him for every chain
   That made us free again,
      Cords that bind closely to God.
                W.J. 57

A GRAIN OF WHEAT

Scripture reading: Matthew 26:55–57

The time is fulfilled, and the kingdom of God
is at hand; repent, and believe in the gospel.
Mark 1:15

Jesus came to establish His kingdom. That is why He
travelled through the countryside announcing to the people:
"The kingdom of heaven is at hand." It seemed as though it
would begin on Palm Sunday when His people hailed Him,
"Hosanna! Blessed is he who comes in the name of the
Lord." (Mark 11:9). At that time it seemed as though Jesus'
great longing would be fulfilled. It looked as though He
would be able to establish the kingdom that He had talked
about in almost every parable. His disciples were fired
with enthusiasm for this—we can tell from their conversa-
tions to what extent they lived in this expectation. The
Father, Son and Holy Spirit also longed for this kingdom to
be established. It would be the Kingdom of God, the kingdom of love and paradise. Should not Jesus contend with the
Pharisees in order that His kingdom might come? Should He
not fight against them and thwart their influence?

Yes, Jesus did fight so that His kingdom might come, but

not in the way that people expected. He chose a way that seemed foolish, meaningless. He allowed His enemies to undermine His kingdom and finally gave Himself into their hands. He let Himself be bound and taken prisoner. Who would acclaim a prisoner as ruler of a kingdom? It was hard for people to believe that Jesus could establish His kingdom in this way. His royal name became a name of abuse. He was ridiculed. The moment He was arrested, the message of His kingdom seemed to disintegrate. The fact that a few days earlier He had been hailed as King was obliterated. It no longer seemed believable that thousands had looked forward to His kingdom. All that Jesus could see was a grave. Buried in it was His most cherished treasure: the coming of the Kingdom of God.

He, who should have been crowned King by His people, was soon laid in a tomb. It is an eternal truth that the Kingdom of God, the kingdom of love, can only come through chains, disgrace and death. It is the same way as that of grain of wheat that dies in the dark night. After the process of decay it becomes a sturdy young plant and brings forth fruit a thousandfold. This way of Jesus is the only way for those who wish to help build the Kingdom of God. There no other way.

My Lord Jesus,

For my sake You are standing in fetters and chains. You are radiant in Your suffering. I worship and adore You. Ruler, standing in fetters, the whole enslaved world bow down at Your feet to thank You for bearing its chains. Host of Your servants hail You and join in jubilation, for You have released them—You have saved them!

Indeed our fettered Saviour has set us free from the law of sin and death. Love bound in chains! How wonderful is this love!

MAJESTIC IN SUFFERING

Scripture reading: John 18:6–12

He who comes from above is above all; he who is of the earth belongs to the earth, and of the earth he speaks; he who comes from heaven is above all.

John 3:31

Jesus was able to act majestically at the time of His arrest, because He was willing to suffer. Whoever submits to suffering has a royal quality. Whoever cannot submit is a miserable, wretched creature, like the disciples before the crucifixion. It was their refusal to face suffering that made the disciples cowards. For this reason they all fled and Peter was shamed by a maid. The contrast between Jesus and the disciples can nowhere be seen so clearly as in suffering. Before they faced the ordeal, the difference was not nearly so obvious. Jesus accomplished great deeds, but the disciples could do this also. The difference was probably in Jesus' power to raise people from the dead. But the moment He began to suffer, it became manifest that Jesus and His disciples lived in two different worlds. Jesus came from above and they came from below. They could not endure suffering, but Jesus could. He could therefore step forward majestically when the band of soldiers arrived, saying, "Let these men go. Shall I not drink the cup?" In this manner He proved His kingship.

Those who bear their suffering out of love and devotion to Jesus are truly kings. They are full of power and glory. These are His disciples who heed His call, "Come, follow Me!" Therefore they win victory over their suffering.

O Jesus, vainly did You yearn
For one who would in pity turn;
If I but one soul had cast a thought
What comfort this to You had brought.

Let me be now that soul I pray,
Your pain relieve and soothe this day,
And step by step with You keep pace,
O Father, grant to me this grace.

I long to share Your cross so sore,
Alone I'll leave You nevermore;
As You to suffering once were wed,
So let me now that pathway tread.

W.J. 71.

Lord Jesus Christ,

I humble myself before You and feel ashamed. You were utterly obedient and submissive to the Father's will. You let them bind Your hands and lead You to agonizing suffering. Yet I, a sinner, so often will not go where You want to lead me, even though You lead me in love. When the way has seemed too hard for me, I have not given You my hand and let You bind it to Yours. But now I surrender to You, Lord Jesus. "Here are my hands. Take them. I want to trust the Father's love. He has planned my ways in love. So lead me as You will and where You will. I want to go with You. I want to be Your prisoner, the prisoner of Your love."

NO SYMPATHY

Scripture reading: Mark 14:43–46, 50

Take your share of suffering as a good soldier of Christ Jesus.

2 Timothy 2:3

Can we imagine how forsaken Jesus must have felt when He was taken prisoner and suddenly found Himself alone, in disgrace and misery? Forsaken! Yes, betrayed by someone close to Him, by one of His twelve disciples with whom He had spent three years of His life! Forsaken by the eleven who should have been on fire, surrounding their Master with love at the time of His arrest! They should have soothed His heart-ache with their steadfastness. Forsaken—or so it seemed—by the Father also! In Gethsemane He had called to the Father as one separated by distance and darkest night, tempted and surrounded by all the powers of hell.

If only the words that Jesus spoke to His disciples would pierce our hearts, "The hour is coming when you will leave me alone." (John 16:32). The Bible report of the arrest adds, "They all forsook him and fled." True of the distant past and also the present! Where are the disciples who are willing to go on trial with Him? Who is willing to be judged? Who goes to Calvary to die with Jesus? Many want Jesus to be "for them" but they do not want to be "with Jesus" when He is in distress, imprisonment and death. The Apostle Paul often wrote on this theme. We isolate Jesus today, just as His disciples did long ago.

This is Jesus' sorrow. He has scarcely any disciples who are willing to travel the path of suffering "with Him". Indeed He has scarcely any disciples who allow their will to be bound to the Father's will. Very few will accompany Jesus into poverty, disgrace, lowliness, and suffering in body and soul. Jesus, bound in chains, stands before us and waits for us to say:

With You the cross's way I'll go,
With You I'll share its pain and woe,
With You go into darkness.
With You I will one day arise,
Be throned with You in paradise,
With You I am united.

Lord Jesus, I worship and praise You,

for freely surrendering Your will to man's will and letting him bind You, although You are his Lord and Creator.

I thank You for doing such a thing for us, to free us from our self-will. Let us be subject to those whom You have appointed as our superiors, even if they are overbearing. Help us to understand that in obeying them, we are humbling ourselves beneath Your powerful hand. Make us willing to obey You through them.

Lord Jesus, I worship and praise You,

Lord of the world, for submitting to arrest and capture by man whom You created. I thank You for suffering so that I may be transformed. I will place my hand in Yours and say, "Where You go I will go." I will follow You along Your way of the cross. This will bring me into a close relationship with You.

I worship You for Your love. Your great love for us made You leave the Father and deliver Yourself into the hands of men. You did this to teach us to reach out and grasp Your hand.

DEFEAT?

Scripture reading: Matthew 26:50b–56

Was it not necessary that the Christ should suffer these things and enter into his glory?
Luke 24:26

There is one thing that the arrest shows us. When Jesus surrendered Himself and became physically powerless, He received the greatest spiritual authority. His hands were bound so that He could not use them. Yet, with His hands nailed to the cross, He accomplished the greatest deed of all time. On the cross He accomplished our redemption. When Jesus was arrested, His disciples lost their confidence in Him. Jesus had told them on the way to the Garden of Gethsemane that they would all fall away. Why? Because He did not act as they thought He would, in power and glory, but in weakness and impotence.

We too experience this. We ask Jesus to prove His power in times of sickness or financial or family problems, in emotional conflicts and temptations. Yet Jesus seems to be impotent. It appears that His hands are bound. He is silent when we cry, "Show us Your power, Lord Jesus Christ." The situation is the same as it was at the arrest. There He employed no words of power to make the earth open and swallow up the soldiers. Yet the hours of His passion were hours laden with the greatest power—power to redeem the whole world. Love that endures, suffers in silence, has power over all things. But this power will be revealed only in *His* own time.

When Jesus appears impotent with His hands bound and He does not come to our aid, He has a very special purpose. He is entreating us, "Do not lose your confidence in Me now. Show Me your trust and faithfulness. When I do not come to your immediate aid and you cannot understand Me, still have faith in Me. Wait for Me to bring you the help and the solution that you need. You must believe this delay to be

39

necessary so that I can accomplish more for you than if I had answered immediately. Expect something special in this situation."

Strength arises out of weakness, light out of darkness, a glorious victory and resurrection out of defeat and apparent loss. Who does believe this? Who does trust Jesus when He seems to be bound with chains? Jesus searches for souls who will not lose their confidence in Him when He veils His power. He longs for souls who trust Him to reveal His power in His own time. He yearns for those who believe that in the end, the answer will be even more wonderful than they anticipated. Jesus seeks disciples who follow the path of suffering and endurance in the knowledge that glory comes from suffering and victory from apparent loss.

Jesus went the way of the Lamb, enduring everything in silence. But this way of bondage has become ennobled, because it was followed by the King of all kings. Jesus will bring victory out of defeat also for all those who will accompany Him. Here on earth they will be granted great power and above they will be seated on thrones.

Lord Jesus,

I worship You because, to save sinners, You let men bind and fetter You. So often we do not desire the power that comes through stillness. In our selfwill, we rush around, trying feverishly to accomplish much with nothing but our own strength. Help us to listen to Your voice and receive strength from You. We worship You for permitting men to bind Your hands and put an end to Your active ministry. We thank You for going the way of suffering. Your silent acceptance of all that was inflicted upon You has given us an example for all times:

The way of the Lamb is the way of victory.

The way of love, that endures suffering, is the way of power that will set many free.

Purest Lamb, You let men bind You,
So may souls to You be bound,
Faithful, true, may they continue
Only You to circle round.
Each one give himself completely,
Dedicate to You his will,
Like a child, obey You freely,
Only Your desires fulfil.

SUFFERING LOVE

Scripture reading: Matthew 26:47, 50–54

When they came to the place of which God told him, Abraham built an altar there, and laid the wood in order, and bound Isaac his son, and laid him on the altar, upon the wood. Then Abraham put forth his hand, and took the knife to slay his son.

Genesis 22:9, 10

The world has no idea how much it cost the Father to give up His Son. There is not a single human soul who can imagine what it meant to Him. Probably it inflicted a wound in His heart which will burn forever like the wounds of His Son. Abraham bound his son with loving hands. No doubt he looked at him with tender, fatherly love, to comfort him. But God stood apart and let His Son be bound by His enemies. They did not bind Him lovingly, as a father would. They fell upon Him like a pack of wolves descending on the prey. A dark shadow must have fallen upon the Father's heart—for the Father and Son are one. The Son was surrounded by evil hordes who led Him captive.

All of this the Father watched. He suffered with His Son in

a deep unity of love. Who could be more closely united than the Holy Trinity—Father, Son and Holy Spirit? One thought, one will, one love and now one in suffering! Who can comprehend? The Godhead separated! The Son was delivered up to another power, to the hands of hell. But still the Godhead was at one—more than ever before. One in love, desirous to suffer and be parted for our sake.

Suffering together in love is the strongest bond of unity. Should it not be victorious? It will indeed be victorious, even in apparent defeat. When the God of love was taken captive, others were set free. The suffering love of God in fetters possesses great power. This power will open doors, burst chains and lead the captives of death out of bondage into the kingdom of love.

There was one freedom which the enemy could not take away from Jesus—the freedom to love. For love, Jesus suffered willingly for those He created. In the hour of capture heaven sang of the love which chose to endure suffering in order to open the kingdom of love and real freedom. The true disciples of Jesus, who have willingly borne suffering out of their love for Him, will enter this kingdom.

Now fettered those hands which such power did wield,
Those hands that so gently once aided and healed
Are laden with chains, they can only be still,
Which never did evil, but only God's will.

O hands of my Saviour, O hands of my King,
Because they wore fetters salvation did bring.
O let me now bless them and praise them today,
That won for me freedom and heaven for aye.

W.J. 55

Praise and glory be to You, my Saviour in chains, my King who was stripped of power. O Love in fetters, how poor and

42

powerless You became for us. Eternal majesty of heaven, Ruler of all the earth, You were bound like a Lamb that is led to slaughter. Yet You are the victorious Lord!

Praise and glory be to You, the eternal King! You surrendered Your freedom, so that we, the servants of sin, might become free men for ever. You set us free to become children in Your Father's house. You surrendered Your will to the Father in childlike love, that we too might willingly obey Him. You emptied Yourself completely of Your supernatural power. You let Your helping hands be bound in order to bind us to You in love. To You be praise and glory eternally!

THE TRIAL

And they led Jesus to the high priest; and all the chief priests and the elders and the scribes were assembled. And Peter had followed him at a distance, right into the courtyard of the high priest; and he was sitting with the guards, and warming himself at the fire. Now the chief priests and the whole council sought testimony against Jesus to put him to death; but they found none. For many bore false witness against him, and their witness did not agree. And some stood up and bore false witness against him, saying, "We heard him say, 'I will destroy this temple that is made with hands and in three days I will build another, not made with hands'." Yet not even so did their testimony agree. And the high priest stood up in the midst, and asked Jesus, "Have you no answer to make? What is it that these men testify against you?" But he was silent and made no answer. Again the high priest asked him, "Are you the Christ, the Son of the Blessed?" And Jesus said, "I am; and you will see the Son of man sitting at the right hand of Power, and coming with the clouds of heaven." And the high priest tore his mantle and said, "Why do we still need witnesses? You have heard his blasphemy. What is your decision?" And they all condemned him as deserving death. And some began to spit on him and to cover his face and to strike him, saying to him, "Prophesy!" And the guards received him with blows.

And as soon as it was morning the chief priests, with the elders and scribes, and the whole council held a consultation; and they bound Jesus and led him away and delivered him to Pilate. And Pilate asked him, "Are you the King of the Jews?" And he answered him, "You have said so." And the chief priests accused him of many things. And Pilate again asked him, "Have you no answer to make? See how many charges they bring against you." But Jesus made no further answer, so that Pilate wondered.

Now at the feast he used to release for them one prisoner whom they asked. And among the rebels in prison, who had committed murder in the insurrection, there was a man called Barabbas. And the crowd came up and began to ask Pilate to do as he was wont to do for them.

And he answered them, "Do you want me to release for you the King of the Jews?" For he perceived that it was out of envy that the chief priests had delivered him up. But the chief priests stirred up the crowd to have him release for them Barabbas instead. And Pilate again said to them, "Then what shall I do with the man whom you call the King of the Jews?" And they cried out again, "Crucify him." And Pilate said to them, "Why, what evil has he done?" But they shouted all the more, "Crucify him." So Pilate, wishing to satisfy the crowd, released for them Barabbas; and having scourged Jesus, he delivered him to be crucified.

Mark 14:53–65; 15:1–15.

Jesus, Jesus, Lord of all things
Stands before the judgment seat.
Bend, proud earth, in shame and sorrow
Humbly at your Maker's feet,
Mourn that He, the Lord almighty,
Is condemned by human spite;
See! The sun and stars are darkened,
Veiled before that dreadful sight.

Jesus, who can ever measure
All Your suffering as You stand
Patiently before Your judges?
Who Your torture understand?
Who express Your pain and anguish,
As You are with sin made one,
When unrighteous judges sentence
You, the Judge and perfect Man?

W.J. 61

IN THE COURT OF LIES

Scripture reading: Mark 14:60–65

But because I tell the truth, you do not believe
me. Which of you convicts me of sin? If I tell
the truth, why do you not believe me?
John 8:45–46

These scenes from Jesus' trial read like a drama. Caiaphas
shouted. He was beside himself with rage. This indicated his
desire to drown his troubled conscience. The accusations
which were brought against Jesus seemed to be true. They
were facts. He had broken their Sabbath laws. He had insulted
the Pharisees by calling them a "brood of vipers". He had
associated with tax collectors and sinners. He had broken
the custom, by speaking to women who were strangers to
Him. He had allowed women to provide for His needs and
had let them accompany Him on His journeys through the
country. But the real reason for the Pharisees' rage was that
they did not want to accept God's judgment. They could not
forgive Jesus for humiliating them with public reproof. But
in their indignation they did not charge Him with this, "You
hurt us, You dishonoured us . . ." No, they were hypocrites.
They disguised their hatred by attacking His teaching. They
did not see the impurity in their hearts. They blinded themselves to their ulterior motives.

This often happens with us too. We judge others but are
blind to our own sin. Religious people are especially in
danger of becoming hypocrites. How often have we condemned other Christians who are trying to take their discipleship seriously, by saying that they are fanatical? When
we criticize others, claiming that they are not teaching
sound doctrines, we usually have an ulterior motive.
Perhaps we do not want to be judged for our own

47

lukewarmness. It humiliates us to see that someone else has more spiritual life than we have and that his work is more successful than ours.

When we condemn others, we must seek the ulterior motive in our own hearts. Then our eyes will become aware of our own sins. We will otherwise be judging Jesus anew, in our neighbours, just as the religious people of His time tore His reputation to shreds.

Who will not be judged here,
Will one day be judged there.
Sins will come to light
In that dazzling light,
For those who escaped judgment here
Eternal just judgment will bear,
And the judgment by which we have judged,
Is the judgment by which we'll be judged,
For eternity.

CONFLICTING VERDICTS

Scripture reading: Matthew 27:15–23

I lie in the midst of lions that greedily devour the sons of men; their teeth are spears and arrows, their tongues sharp swords.

Psalm 57

It is not hard to understand why Jesus was called to trial before Herod. This man was governed by hell, even during his lifetime. Yet he was the one who declared Jesus innocent. It is also not hard to understand why Jesus had to come before Pilate. He had no knowledge of the true God. He was heathen who served false gods. Yet he too did not dare to declare Jesus guilty. He was uncertain, and when his wife warned him, "Have nothing to do with that righteous man!" he was afraid to condemn him to death.

Who dared to condemn Jesus—to condemn God? It is frightening to realize that it was the religious people—Annas and Caiaphas. With great self-assurance they belittled Jesus and finally Caiaphas tore his robe and condemned Him to death. Does this not show his belief that he was quite justified in passing sentence upon Jesus? The trial of Jesus was conducted with an arrogance that should make us shudder with fear. How can people dare to rise up against God and condemn Him to death? Only boundless arrogance could have allowed this to happen. It is not the godless and agnostics who behave in this way. It is the religious people—both then and now. Should that not frighten us into crying out to God, "Help me to be cautious. Let me not judge You also by judging Your disciples who do Your work. Prevent me from committing this great sin."?

Lord Jesus,

I humble myself before You, because I have not taken Your Word seriously. You have commanded us plainly: First remove the beam from your own eye, before you remove the speck from your neighbour's eye. Yet I have passed judgment upon others. I have accused and wounded them without humbling myself for my own sin, before God and man, although mine was much greater than theirs. Oh, forgive me for being such a hypocrite! I thought I was following You, but I was actually following the enemy, who is the accuser. Forgive me for grieving You so much. Be gracious to me, a sinner. I believe in Your redemption. I trust in Your victory over my critical spirit.

A SILENT LAMB

Scripture reading: Mark 14:53-59

He was oppressed, and he was afflicted, yet he opened not his mouth; like a lamb that is led to the slaughter, and like a sheep that before its shearers is dumb, so he opened not his mouth.

Isaiah 53:7

From all sides, critical thoughts and words flew like arrows at Jesus. How could it have been any different? He had to occupy the place that we deserved. We should be in the place of the accused eternally. How dreadful must hell be for those who have judged others here. To the extent that we have judged others, we will be judged. The accusations of people and evil spirits will descend upon us. We will never be able to rest day or night. The countless words of judgment that we have spoken against others will return and pierce us, for we will be in the kingdom of the accuser.

Because we constantly judge others, Jesus had to stand in the bitter place of the accused. He did it to rescue us from the hand of the accuser and to ransom us from his kingdom of hell. Not only was He torn to pieces publicly in front of four judges. No! Throughout His ministry He was surrounded by groups of people who were judging Him. The trial had to go on and on, because our judgment of others does not come to an end. Our sin of criticism vented its fury on Jesus, because no one else would bear countless accusations. We usually react against even the slightest reproach. No one wants to be judged, so Jesus took all accusations upon Himself. Even if for once we are silent, we usually have critical thoughts. For the first time in the history of the world there was Someone who would accept all the arrows of judgment that were fired at Him. He did not judge or retaliate even in thought. He wanted to accept all ur accusations in order to put an end to judgment and criticism.

Who claims His offer of redemption? He offers salvation rom one of the most serious sins. Woe to him who turns own His offer and persists in the sin of judgment. The vords of Scripture are true. "Judge not, that you be not idged." (Matthew 7:1). "For judgment is without mercy ɔ one who has shown no mercy." (James 2:13).

HE SAME TODAY

Scripture reading: Luke 22:66–71

If I had not done among them the works which no one else did, they would not have sin; but now they have seen and hated both me and my Father. It is to fulfil the word that is written in their law, "They hated me without a cause."

John 15:24, 25

: is often taken for granted that Jesus' passion, with its tations of the cross, occurred only once. We are apt to hink that the arrest and the crowning with thorns and so on ame to an end, once and for all. But the rejection, the atred, the betrayal, the denial, the abuse and the other vickednesses were not a one-time occurrence. Those whom Ie created continue to do these things to Him today. Jesus emains the same for all time. That is why His loving heart uffers just as much today when people oppose Him and eject His love. Long ago, God's creatures put Jesus in the ock and hurled reproaches and accusations at Him. Today ve still do it. Thousands of accusing voices reach His heart ay by day. They blame God for wars and the chastenings in 1eir lives. They even criticize Him for the things that do not appen to suit them, such as bad weather. Arrows of hatred are constantly shot at Jesus, piercing His heart. Whole nations reject Him. Jesus loves us so much that He gave His life for us, yet no one has ever been accused and hated as much as He. He endured all the suffering of the trial in order to redeem us from judgment. Could it be that all the accusations which reach His heart today, hurt Him much more than His trial, because each accusation is a rejection of His redemption? This means that every complaint we make against God, about the way He leads us, is doubly a sin. Lord, let me be fearful when I think how God was accused by sinners and condemned to death!

O Holy Spirit, give me eyes to see Jesus' sorrows, both then and now. Show me how deeply I grieve Him when I judge others. There is nothing that hurts love more than harshness, criticism and hatred. Show me, Lord Jesus, that my judgment and rebellion against others is really rebellion against You, because these people are Your instruments when they wrong me. You would use them to make me humble. Let me do everything possible to prevent Your suffering the pain of the many critical barbs shot at You by mankind. Let me bring balm to Your heart today by loving those who have hurt me. Let me do good to them, out of love for You.

We are all such good defence witnesses for ourselves. When we are criticized we always have a ready answer. In this way we reveal the pride in our hearts. When Jesus was on trial, even the depths of His heart revealed nothing but humility in Him. Jesus is the only One who has passed through every trial unblemished. In those hours we can see the truth of His words, "I am gentle and lowly in heart." What can be said about us and our behaviour when we are put on trial?

O man, accuse yourself today,
Then for God's grace you've paved the way.

Lord Jesus,

I humble myself before You. You had to take the place of the accused for me, because I cannot accept the slightest reproach. Forgive my boundless pride. I am always condemning others and yet I cannot bear the slightest blame myself. Forgive me for causing You infinite grief with my criticisms.

I thank You because Your Spirit of truth shows me my sin so that I can confess it to You and to men. I believe, "If we confess our sins. You, who are faithful and just, will forgive our sins—and cleanse us from all unrighteousness,"—even from the spirit of judgment.

SINNERS ENTHRONED

Scripture reading: Luke 23:13–19

Do you not know that the saints will judge the world?

1 Corinthians 6:2

Jesus submitted to a trial by men. For our sake He became the Accused. If we believe in Him who let Himself be judged for us, the accuser can no longer accuse us. Now we can rejoice and say, "Jesus was accused in my stead. The accuser no longer has any right over me." What a wonderful gift God has given us! Surely this would have been a great enough gift. But Jesus' loving nature was not satisfied merely with releasing us from the prosecution. His sacrifice includes something even more marvellous. He won for us the right to be enthroned in His Father's kingdom and judge the world with Him. For this end Jesus endured every indictment with joy. That is why He was willing to accept every new accusation levelled at Him. Perhaps when His spirit rejoiced He said, "Now I shall be able to ransom souls from judgment. One day they will sit upon My throne and rule with Me."

Jesus could have been crucified without all these trials. But in His great love He allowed Himself to be judged so often and so harshly, so that one day He might raise us up to be judges of the world. He wants us to be companions in His love through all eternity, sharing His throne with Him. God in His love wishes us to inherit glory and power, although we deserve to be condemned to hell for our sins. Who can understand such love?

IN HIS FOOTSTEPS

Scripture reading: Mark 15:2-5

For to this you have been called, because Christ also suffered for you, leaving you an example that you should follow in his steps. He committed no sin; no guile was found on his lips. When he was reviled, he did not revile in return; when he suffered he did not threaten; but he trusted to him who judges justly.

1 Peter 2:21-2

Where can we find disciples who would choose the place of the accused—the place where our Lord, the Son of God stood? Who listens to His call, "If any man would come after me, let him take up his cross" (Matthew 16:24)? This includes the cross of humiliation. We sinners need to let ourselves be humbled by accepting the judgments that we

54

have deserved. If we resist humiliation, we cease to be His disciples. For His disciples allow themselves to be judged and humiliated by others. Whoever walks in this way will be protected from heresies. He will not go astray from the true way. He will not fall into delusion and fanaticism. For when we suffer and are judged, we cannot continue living in self-deception. We recognize ourselves as we are and we realize how wonderful our Lord is. Truly, whoever loves to be judged by Jesus is following the surest road to the City of God.

My Lord Jesus,

Give me the grace to see You in the place of the accused. Let me be so shaken by this sight that I can no longer remain in my judge's seat. Help me to stoop down to the sinner's place and cry out to You, "Judge me! Accuse me! Let Your Holy Spirit show me my resistance to the rebukes of others." Lord Jesus, You accepted the accusations, although You are pure and holy. Let me now, as a sinner, do the same, knowing that through these accusations You are judging me.

My Lord Jesus, I now want to examine myself in Your holy sight. Remind me of the things in my life that have saddened You. It is essential for me to be freed henceforward from my self-righteousness and my spirit of criticism. I ask this as part of my faith. You have redeemed me, by submitting to judgment for me, although You were innocent. I stand on the foundation of Your redemption. I praise Your redeeming blood and believe in its power.

> O Lamb of God at You I'm gazing,
> Awed by meekness so amazing;
> Judged and mocked You silent stood.
>
> Lord, give me such deep repentance,
> That I ever stand in silence
> When accused, condemned and judged.

OUR HUMBLE LORD

Scripture reading: Matthew 26:62–66

I am gentle and lowly in heart.
Matthew 11:29b

Jesus was reviled and insulted with vulgar language. Yet He remained silent. He did not even use a humble defence saying that He had not come to rule, but to serve. Humility does not defend itself. Humility lets itself be judged. Humility abases itself lower and lower beneath every fresh accusation, beneath every fresh ridicule. The louder the shouts of condemnation, the quieter is the humble spirit.

Jesus was silent. His humility was at one with the Father's will. He had ordained that the Son should suffer like a lamb. "When he was reviled, he did not revile in return; when he suffered, he did not threaten." (1 Peter 2:23). Like a lamb, He was silent before His shearers. Humility does not put forward a defence. It does not make excuses. It humbles itself beneath the judgment of another. When it is wronged, it loves the other person, prays for him and blesses him. Love has great power over others. It is the greatest power in heaven and on earth. It is always victorious.

Dear Lord Jesus,
You are the Lamb who was reviled by Your judges and yet You did not revile in return. O Lord and Judge of all the world, I surrender myself to You. I too want to be like a lamb when I am under attack. Help me to realize, from the bottom of my heart, that I am a sinner who deserves to be condemned.

Take my life, Lord; all my being;
To Thee, Judge, myself I'm giving.

Lord accuse and challenge me,
All my sins are known to Thee.

Lord Jesus,

Prevent me from fighting side by side with Your enemies who so wronged You. You forgave them, so I too would forgive others when they wrong me. I want to look upon the wickedness of others with eyes of love. I want to overlook all that is hurtful to me and seek to repay evil with good. Graciously accept my commitment. I commit myself through faith in Your redemption and in a spirit of love and thankfulness for the suffering You endured throughout the trial. Please accept and bless this commitment.

O place of judgment! Wondrous place,
Where God has pardoned sin by grace,
Set free from judging, pride and hate
Which makes us sad and desolate.
O place of full redemption,
Of grace and love's salvation,
From judging spirit I'm set free,
To love all men, as He loves me.

I adore You, O loving Jesus. I worship the love which inspired You to come amongst us sinners and submit to trial by us. Now the accuser, who seeks to condemn us day and night, must finally be silent.

I praise You for Your unending patience and never tiring love that continues to suffer all our accusations and sins of criticism.

I praise You for forbearing to cast out us Christians. You have ransomed us from the sin of criticism through Your passion. But we remain so shameless that we continue to judge others as though You had never endured the torment of the trial.

I praise Your unfathomable love, which is prepared to continue suffering for ungrateful people who do not value Your sacrifice. I praise Your love that entreats us to this day, "Do not judge!"

THE SCOURGING

So when Pilate saw that he was gaining nothing, but rather that a riot was beginning, he took water and washed his hands before the crowd, saying, "I am innocent of this man's blood; see to it yourselves." And all the people answered, "His blood be on us and on our children!" Then he released for them Barabbas, and having scourged Jesus, delivered him to be crucified.

Matthew 27:24–26

Heaven bows itself in wonder,
Angels, awestruck, veil their sight!
Weep, O heavens, don your mourning,
Darkened be the source of light!
God's own Son is bound for scourging,
Stripped and naked, to the post,
There the cruel stripes awaiting
On the way to shameful death.

W.J. 64

AN UNMISTAKABLE WARNING

Scripture reading: John 18:36—19:1

For God has done what the law, weakened by
the flesh, could not do: sending his own Son in
the likeness of sinful flesh and for sin, he condemned sin in the flesh.

Without the shedding of blood there is no forgiveness of sins.

Romans 8:3; Hebrews 9:22b

Jesus was the delight of all heaven, of angels and men. The
heavenly hosts broke into paeans of praise whenever they
saw Him. Then because of our sin He became an object of
horror—abhorred by all. He was so despised that "men hid
their faces" from Him (Isaiah 53:3). Jesus, tied to the pillar
and scourged—a dreadful sight! If only we could see ourselves reflected in this—with our sins of impurity and lust.
We deserve to be disfigured like this for our sins. If only we
would allow the horror of this situation to bring us to repentance. Then we would accept His redemption from our
sins. How can this terrible vision leave us unmoved? The
Holy One of God was not just taking our part as a play
actor. He actually took our sin upon Himself and accepted
the punishment which we sinners deserve. In view of this
can we still persevere in the same sin?

"If you were blind, you would have no guilt." (John 9:41).
Is Jesus' cry not still the same today? We can see His
suffering and yet we can remain as cold as stone. Often,
indeed, we persist in our old sins of lust and immorality. We
remain in bondage to our flesh, to food, to comfort and to
sleep. We hold His suffering in contempt. We pierce His
heart deeper than did the people of Israel. That is why we
will be judged more severely, if we do not turn from our

ways and repent. Let us gaze at Him whom we have wounded with our sin, and weep. The scourging He suffered at the pillar was caused by our sin alone. We should lament as we would lament at the loss of a first-born child.

Such repentance would make us willing to submit to God's powerful hand when we are stricken with illness. Suffering can purify us from our unclean desires. "Whoever has suffered in the flesh has ceased from sin." (1 Peter 4:1).

O son of man, admit your sin,
Consider what you do to Him,
You scourge Your Lord and Maker!
You think it was those soldier men,
The priests and Romans, only them,
Who made our dear Lord suffer?

But no! It happens still today,
Their sin and guilt we too display,
We still reject the Saviour.
Our sin brings suffering, grief and pain,
He feels those scourging blows again,
Whenever lust is victor.

Lord Jesus,

I humble myself before You when I am ill and weak. You had need to visit me with illness so that I could be healed from my uncleansed physical and emotional desires. I humble myself beneath Your mighty hand, for I am a sinner, who needs this chastening of Your love. You have promised me, "Whoever has suffered in the flesh has ceased from sin."

I thank You that through this chastening, You are preparing a new body for my resurrection. You have won this new, immortal body for me through Your scourging, through Your bitter suffering and death. Help me to bear my

61

illness and suffering at one with You, my scourged Saviour, so that through it I shall be renewed.

Our suffering and ailments lead us to consider the picture of Him who suffered for our sin—Jesus. In our suffering let us thank Him. He is the Man of Sorrows who bore all the suffering of the whole world, out of love for us.

I hear a voice lamenting,
A Lamb in agony.
Yes, we are God tormenting,
Who came to set us free.
For us His erring children,
Who were in such dire need,
For us, the chief of sinners,
He bleeds to death indeed.

W.J. 63

SCOURGED FOR OUR SIN

Scripture reading: Luke 23:20–25

Do you not know that if you yield yourselves to any one as obedient slaves, you are slaves of the one whom you obey, either of sin which leads to death, or of obedience which leads to righteousness?

Romans 6:16

God has given us food for nourishment—but craving for food and sleep and the satisfaction of our sensual desires is evil. God has given us people to love—but the desire to cling to people and yearn for their love is also evil. When we take the good things God has created and pursue them with lust and passion, we become enslaved by them. We are surrendering to Satan.

When we feel we need something so badly we cannot live without it, we have become slaves to our desires. We would soon adopt sinful means to achieve our ends. Then we would be ensnared by hell, even if we confessed Jesus' name. When our body is feverishly striving to satisfy its desires, we have some idea of the torments that will await us in hell. The story of the rich man who lived to satisfy his palate illustrates the point for us. (Luke 16). Eternity revealed his bondage to food and drink. Through this desire he suffered anguish with a burning tongue. We need to be set free, if we do not want the fate of the rich man to await us in eternity. Here on earth we must fight to the extreme of shedding blood to resist the sins of bondage. Jesus' blood was shed from hundreds of wounds for our sake. Such is the seriousness of our sins of lust in God's sight.

Lord Jesus,

You know how terribly You suffered during the scourging for my sake. You know the fever in my blood. For a while I can resist my desires. But then they rise up again as if from the dead, with such intensity that I feel as though I shall die, if I do not satisfy them.

My Lord Jesus, sin has a powerful hold over my flesh, but I must be set free from these evil desires. Satan tries to convince me that these desires must be good, because You created them. But they have become corrupt through the fall.

So I commit myself to You today. I renounce the desires of my flesh, which brought You the dreadful torment of scourging. I will no longer seek to satisfy my palate and my desires. With You I shall crucify my flesh, so that my members shall live for sin no more, but only for You and Your righteousness.

LASHED FOR OUR REBELLION

Scripture reading: Luke 23:13-19, 24, 25

His citizens hated him and sent an embassy after him, saying, "We do not want this man to reign over us."

Luke 19:1

Many men are prepared to lay down their lives in war. They know their death will be valued. But people did not want to acknowledge Jesus' life as a sacrifice for the world. The death of the Son of God was not valued. On the contrary, people wanted to get rid of Jesus, because they decided that He was not fit for this earth. They could no longer endure His holiness. They did not want Him to become their King. The crudeness of the soldiers at the scourging showed clearly His rejection by His people: "Away with Him! Away with Him!"

Let us consider this: the scourging of our Lord symbolizes the revolt in our hearts against God, our rebellion against His will. We well know how our hearts rebel when things do not go the way we desire. But what we do not usually realize is that this rebellion is in fact directed at Jesus. It strikes Him just as did the whips at the scourging. The sentiment behind our rebellion is the same as that behind the shout "'Away with this man!' "We do not want this man to reign over us!"

People were quite happy to watch Jesus healing. But when He told them that they must forsake various things, they began to mistrust Him. Instead of realizing that He wanted to release them from their shackles, they mistrusted this command. Instead of realizing that He wanted to give them a new and happier life, they thought that He did not wish them to be happy. They decided that He was demanding ng too much of them, so they rebelled against Him. First in thought, but later in deed—in the scourging.

If we mistrust God's love when He leads us in difficult ways or when He judges us, we too are falling into the sin of scourging Him. We join in this today. We must therefore reform our ways, if we do not want to belong to the party who grieve and torment Jesus' heart. The slightest thought of rebellion lands us on the side of His opponents, even if we do not realize it.

The people shouted, "His blood be on us and on our children!" They meant that they did not mind, if vengeance came upon them. Jesus' answer was overwhelming. Yes, He would let His blood come upon them—but as the blood of forgiveness and reconciliation. When His time comes, His blood will flow over Israel to cleanse and sanctify. How amazing and wonderful is His love! He accepted their words of hatred as a plea and answered with blessing and grace. Certainly His people must first receive judgment. But instead of being separated from Him eternally, they are promised that they will one day recognize Him as their Redeemer. Then they will look on Him whom they have pierced and will repent and be pardoned.

Such mighty power is in His blood! What an incredibly loving response to the hatred of men!

CRUEL WOUNDS BRING SALVATION

Scripture reading: Matthew 27:24–26

The blood of Jesus his Son cleanses us from all sin.

1 John 1:7b

we really believe in Jesus, we cannot bear to contemplate His scourging and yet remain in bondage to our sin. If we give in to unbridled desires to satisfy our palate, to oversleep, or any other excesses, we will hurt Jesus in the same way as those who scourged Him. If these things captivate our thoughts, we hold Him in contempt anew. Jesus let Himself be scourged in order to suffer the full penalty of our unrestrained desires. He set us free. Indeed, we are released absolutely from this stern bondage. His blood streamed forth from countless wounds, to redeem our corrupt blood.

"Who has believed what we have heard?" says Isaiah. "And to whom has the arm of the Lord been revealed?" Those who believe in the powerful results of His suffering, in the power of the redeeming blood that flowed from His wounds at the scourging, will experience the might of His arm. The sight of Jesus being scourged should make us long to be freed from our bondage at all costs. All who cry out to Him for release from enslavement to the appetites of their flesh will experience redemption. But if we cling to our desires, they will keep us from entering the Kingdom of God.

O Jesus, here Thou showest
What love can bear for me.
This path of pain Thou goest
From guilt my soul to free.
Thy body now is tortured
With countless bleeding wounds.
Thou didst in love choose freely
To die, for sin atone.

W.J. 62

My Lord Jesus,
    You see how tightly I am bound and how hard it is to break the hold of my desires. I thank You for the knowledge

that as surely as You submitted to scourging I have been
redeemed from my chains. Your sacrifice is all powerful.
Grant me a patient faith so that I shall not grow weary of
believing, even when I cannot see any sign of Your redemption in my life. Let me stand firm in the assurance that
this battle will not be decided by single defeats or victories,
but by an enduring faith. I will cling to the verse:

"So if the Son makes you free,
you will be free indeed!"

TEMPLES OF GOD

Scripture reading: Mark 15:14, 15

You were bought with a price. So glorify
God in your body.

1 Corinthians 6:20

From now on let us give glory to God in our bodies. We shall
never fully understand the benefits of the new, pure and
wonderful body God has won for us through our Lord Jesus.
At the resurrection it will be pure and unblemished, pos-
sessing divine beauty and glory. Truly, this body will look
like His, as Paul said; He "will change our lowly body to be
like his glorious body, by the power which enables him even
to subject all things to himself." (Philippians 3:21).

It is amazing how much our Lord Jesus achieved for us
through His bitter suffering when He was tied to the pillar
and scourged. All our sins of impurity, from our childhood
onwards, were blotted out. We ourselves could never oblit-
erate them, but if we confess these sins, He will erase them.
Only if we bring them into the light and repent of them, is
the cleansing power of Jesus' blood available to us. So when
we look upon our scourged Saviour, we are confronted with

a decision which we must make. If we want to be forgiven, cleansed, redeemed and prepared for a resurrection body, we must confess our sins of lust and repent of them. We Christians know how terribly the Man of Sorrows suffered to redeem us from sin. We shall therefore receive an even sharper verdict than those responsible for the scourging, if we ignore His grace.

Lord Jesus,

I worship and praise You, O my scourged Saviour, for enduring countless wounds for my sake, on account of my sins of the flesh. The salvation bought by Your wounds will set me free from the sinful desires of my flesh.

I worship and adore You, my Lord Jesus, because You bore the torment of scourging that I should have endured. Since You bore this suffering, my body can become a temple of God again. I can become pure and holy and one day I shall arise in glory.

UNDER THE GUISE OF JUSTICE

Scripture reading: Matthew 27:24–26

Thou hast set our secret sins in the light of thy countenance.

Psalm 90:8

Pilate was responsible for Jesus' scourging, for he it was who handed Him over to the soldiers. It is frightening to see that his behaviour towards Jesus was determined by his desire to avoid criticism. In every decision Pilate considered only himself. Nothing else mattered to him. He did not care what happened to Jesus. His interest lay only in making certain that no one would find fault with him. Pilate wanted to convince his own conscience and demonstrate to the people that he had done his best to protect Jesus from death. So he ordered that He should be scourged instead. Of course Pilate knew how often scourging brought about death. But if Jesus had died, officially it would not have been Pilate's fault, because he had not pronounced the death penalty. It would have been a "mishap" merely, for which the soldiers would have been responsible. We should surely tremble when we look at Pilate. When we make decisions in order to look innocent and blameless, we may become doubly guilty. Pilate caused Jesus great torture, even redoubled torture, through his hesitation. First the scourging and later, when he saw that he had not succeeded, the crucifixion.

How often we deceive ourselves when we do not want to acknowledge ulterior motives. We like to appear pious but we really have only ourselves in mind, not Jesus. We are not especially interested in loving Him, living for Him and bringing Him joy. How often we harbour impure motives. We can even say evil things in a very pious manner.

We may enjoy thoughts that seem to be good, although they come from evil roots. Hypocritical thinking caused Jesus' scourging. This can still hurt and wound Him in a similar way today.

Patient as a lamb He suffers,
'Gainst their frenzy, quiet and still,
Bows Himself beneath the scourging,
Lets them use Him as they will.
Hides His face all marred by torment
Of the body, mind and soul,
Yet through every wound the scourge makes
Pours His love to make us whole.

W.J. 64

LOVE HEALS

Scripture reading: John 11:49–53; 19:1

The glory which thou hast given me I have given to them, that they may be one even as we are one, I in them and thou in me, that they may become perfectly one, so that the world may know that thou hast sent me and hast loved them even as thou hast loved me.

John 17:22–23

When we look at the spiritual Body of our Lord Jesus, His Church, we can truly see how much it resembles the scourged body of Jesus. It is torn apart and wounded, because the members often fight against one another. Do we want to continue to scourge Jesus like this? Only His love can heal our wounds. In a similar way, the wounds of His Body, the Church, can only be healed by love. For the sake of His scourging, let us ask Him to give us this love. It will enable us to love even our enemies. If we receive wounds on the way, let us be prepared to bear them. We can only heal the wounds in His Body by bearing wounds.

Oh, if only we would praise the blood He shed and call upon its healing power to mend the divisions in His Body, the Church. He suffered for the sake of His Church, that it might be united in love. If only we could recognize our scourged Saviour in the wounded Body of His Church—wounded in strife and envy! When we partake of Holy Communion, let us include all our brothers and sisters in our prayers. His blood has healing power. Through the wounds of the Lamb of God, unity will be granted.

My Lord Jesus, hear my prayer:

Let me give You, the Man of Sorrows covered with wounds, the proper response to Your scourging. Surely Your wounds should inspire me to do everything I can to soothe and bind them. May this be my constant answer to Your scourging from now on. Dissension and quarrelling have filled Your Body—Your Church—with wounds and divisions. Because I share this guilt, may Your scourging inspire me to do all I can to soothe these wounds also.

I commit myself to You, O wounded Lamb. I want to help bind the wounds of Your Body and heal them through a love that also embraces all the members of Your Body. Let me learn to esteem others more highly than myself. Then I shall not be piously meditating upon the scourging You suffered, while I add to the pain by my unkind attitude towards others.

THE CROWNING WITH THORNS

And the soldiers plaited a crown of thorns, and put it on his head, and arrayed him in a purple robe; they came up to him, saying, "Hail, King of the Jews!" and struck him with their hands. Pilate went out again, and said to them, "Behold, I am bringing him out to you, that you may know that I find no crime in him." So Jesus came out, wearing the crown of thorns and the purple robe. Pilate said to them, "Here is the man!"

John 19:2–5

Midst shouts of derision men crown God with thorns;
Self-righteous and bitter, mankind its Lord scorns.
Deprived of all honour, the Saviour stands there,
Ne'er such gross injustice occurred anywhere.

DISGRACED IN THE FATHER'S SIGHT

Scripture reading: Mark 15:16–19

Remember, O Lord, how thy servant i
scorned; how I bear in my bosom the insult
of the peoples, with which thy enemies taunt
O Lord, with which they mock the footstep
of thy anointed.

Psalm 89:50, 5

Those whom God created ridiculed and scorned their Cre
ator, the only Son. They almost broke His heart. He thirste
for the love and respect of His creatures. Probably He coul
only pray: "My heart is broken with the insults I have re
ceived, so that I am in despair." The Father is one with th
Son. His heart too was probably breaking. He had to watc
His Son so disgraced, sitting on a fool's throne. The dreadfu
thorn wreath pierced His head and blood was streamin
down from all the wounds. The Father saw evil fists beatin
His Son's face, until it became swollen and quite unrecogniz
able. What a terrible sight this must have been for ever
person who still respected human dignity. What agony i
must have caused God, who was His Father! The Father'
heart was really breaking with grief.

His eyes looked down to earth, searching out one wh
would stand by His Son. Did He not have twelve disciple
and a large group of adherents? But they were all far awa
No one was with Him, who could have said to Him in thi
hour, "Nevertheless, You truly are the Son of God and th
King of all kings!" How much these words would hav
soothed the Father and the Son during this bitter hour o
temptation beneath the crown of thorns! How muc
strength and encouragement the Son would have received
but one man would have spoken them. But His followe
remained silent. Only scornful voices inspired by the enem

74

reached the ears of Father and Son. Wild accusations, derision and ridicule filled the air, incited by the prince of hell himself.

Who can understand the Father's agony? His only Son, His beloved Son, whom He gave as King to His people, was rejected. For years His people had yearned for a king. They had even demanded one from God! But, what kind of kings had they hailed in exultation? Most of them were utterly worthless. They exploited their people and led them into corruption. Then Jesus came, a King so different from the others. He was filled with radiance, glory and majesty, with beauty, power and wisdom. He was filled with love for His people. Yet the people of Israel did not accept Him as their King. They did not want His reign of love, because it was coupled with truth, which showed them their true nature. The Son of the Father, their God, the Lord of hosts, had always loved them. He had "led them with cords of compassion, with the bands of love." (Hosea 11:4). This was the One they were rejecting. Nothing the chosen people did could have grieved the Father's heart more than this. Should we not bring joy to the Father's heart now by accepting Jesus as our Lord and King? We should not withdraw a single area of our life from His dominion. We should let Him rule us completely. After we have observed Jesus, so ridiculed and scorned, should we not throw ourselves in the dust before Him? Should we not humble ourselves beneath His mighty hand and let Him lead and chasten us? In this way we can honour Him.

THE CRUCIAL TEST

Scripture reading: Matthew 27:27–30

Now is the judgment of this world, now shall
the ruler of this world be cast out. The ruler of
this world is coming. He has no power over
me.

John 12:31; 14:30b

Lucifer wanted to rob God of His crown and His throne.
This was Lucifer's great desire. But he did not succeed. The
angelic prince of light was cast down into the depths. As the
prince of this world, he built himself a throne, to stand next
to God's throne. He did everything he could to make his
subjects, the children of this world, go the same way as
himself. He tried to make them reach out for God's throne.
Men were eager to rule, no matter what it might cost. Each
one, no matter how small his territory might be, wanted
power and respect. They donned crowns, awarded themselves titles and honours and built themselves thrones.

When the Son of God came to earth, He did not compete
for honour. He walked the earth humbly. As an Infant He
lived with the animals in a stable. As a grown Man He practised His craft in quietness and seclusion, although He had
such mighty powers. His last three years on earth were spent
wandering through the countryside in poverty, preaching
and healing. His needs were supplied by women. He was
surrounded by poor, untrained disciples. He did not have the
same education as the Scribes and Pharisees and He was not
of their class. He was nothing but a poor lay preacher. It was
this humility that showed the enemy His majestic power.
Satan does not have this power, because it stems only from
humility. It infuriated him and he was determined to destroy it. He wanted to snatch away Jesus' invisible crown of
humility and trample it in the dust, so that he alone would
have a crown and be able to rule. He planted this desire in

76

the hearts of the people also, especially in the hearts of the Scribes and Pharisees. Adam and Eve fell, because they wanted to be like God. Since that time all the children of the world have had this urge within them, to rule and make themselves important. But the crown of humility was the only crown Jesus wore on earth. Would the enemy succeed in removing it, if he provoked Him enough with humiliations and ridicule? Or would Jesus still prove to be gentle and lowly? If so, the victory would be His and He would draw a whole host into this kingdom of humility. So the battle began. Satan entered the fight with all his hosts. The Scribes and Pharisees, joined by the crowds of people, strove to deprive this divine Lord and King of His honour, dignity and power. His people, for whom He had done so much during the past three years, came together to deride Him under the crown of thorns.

Satan was intent upon evil. He thought the crown of thorns would goad Jesus beyond endurance so that He would surely lose His humility. He thought He could conquer Him with the bitter suffering that the crown of thorns would bring to His body, soul and spirit. But what happened when Jesus was crowned with the crown of thorns? Satan was beaten! Jesus won this war and the crown of humility shone more brightly than ever upon His head. Humbly He submitted to all the disgrace and derision. Silently He loved those who beat Him. The rays of the crown of thorns have brought many people under their dominion since then. They have inspired them to discard their crowns of pride and enter the kingdom of God, the kingdom based on love and humility. Jesus' humble love was victorious beneath the crown of thorns. It proved to be stronger than Satan's power. In our lives also, Satan and all the evil that others bring upon us will only be conquered by humble love.

A SERVANT OF ALL

Scripture reading: John 19:2, 3

> Jesus called them to him and said, "You know
> that the rulers of the Gentiles lord it over
> them, and their great men exercise authority
> over them. It shall not be so among you; but
> whoever would be great among you must be
> your servant, and whoever would be first
> among you must be your slave."
>
> Matthew 20:25–27

During the Lenten season we sing the song "O sacred Head,
sore wounded" in remembrance of what was done to Jesus
long ago. Do we understand how we crown Him with a
crown of thorns daily with our love of power and our desire
for attention and recognition?

Do we want to be dependent upon others at work and
obey them? Do we want a position where we have to be
subject to others? We do not realize that when we seek recognition, we are proclaiming that Jesus is dead. If He were
alive for us, we would recognize Him as our Lord. Because
Jesus lives today and loves us, He still suffers because of our
desire for attention and recognition. He suffers as long as
those whom His heart loves, do not return to Him. He suffers
when He is rejected. He suffers when His requests are not
fulfilled. Jesus, eternal Love, suffers, because all His enemies
are not yet lying at His feet. He still has to wait for this to
happen. The letter to the Hebrews tells us this about the
High Priest. (Hebrews 10:13).

So Jesus suffers on as He did during His passion on earth
and His followers do not realize that Jesus is waiting for
them just as He waited for His disciples long ago. He is
waiting for us to stand at His side. He is waiting for us to
look upon Him crowned with the crown of thorns and let
ourselves be humbled willingly. Ever since the Son of God
crowned with thorns, became the most despised and re

cted of all men, He has been calling to us, "Follow Me!"
ver since Jesus' mock coronation with thorns, it has
ecome the greatest privilege for us to be reviled and ridi-
led for His sake. For He said that if they "utter all kinds of
vil against you falsely, on my account, rejoice and be glad,
or your reward is great in heaven." (Matthew 5: 11–12).
Vill you follow Jesus?

O Lord, the thorns that pierced You,
With pains that still continue,
Were caused by pride, my haughty pride.

The thorn wounds, sore and bleeding,
Are evermore repeating;
My sin of judging wounds You still.

The thorns that mock my Saviour,
That scorn His holy honour,
Reveal my vain conceit and pride.

ord Jesus,
Forgive me for trying, consciously or unconsciously, to
ake a name for myself and to receive honour from others.
orgive me for living without the slightest relationship to
ou and Your suffering. I knew that You were crowned
ith the crown of thorns and that man dishonoured You.
et I went on seeking my own honour instead of being on
re to see Your name magnified. I commit myself to You
day. From now on I do not want to be worth anything
nong men. I wish my name to be of no account so that
our name may shine forth through my life and the glory
ill be Yours.

It's my self-righteousness and pride that share the blame
For Jesus' wearing purple gown of scorn and shame.

For all my haughtiness and pride He had to pay,
And so they crowned Him with a crown of thorns th‹
day.

O may I deep within the dust, Lord, ever bow,
Because I robbed You of all honour, then and now.

The fruit of the victory that Jesus won when He w‹
crowned with thorns will be granted to the penitent; the‹
will be redeemed from their pride.

But woe to those who fail to repent in view of su‹
suffering! They crown Jesus anew with disgrace and sham‹
Their pride will bind them more tightly to Satan.

I trust the victory of the crown of thorn.
'Twas not in vain You suffered bitter scorn;
  Your pain redeemed me from my pride.

You have redeemed Your child, You set me free,
From pride, self-righteousness and misery;
  You paid the ransom, Lord, for me.

Lord Jesus,

Your humility shone brightly under the crown of thor‹
and You redeemed us to be humble. I will not let You ‹
until You imprint Your humility upon my heart. I want ‹
become like You so that I can help to build Your kingdo‹
the kingdom of humble love. O Lord Jesus, accept my wi‹
ingness to admit that You are right in everything that Y‹
do. Let me now humble myself beneath Your hand and b‹
neath the hands of those who lead me, even if they see‹
overbearing. Grant me Your blessing and the strength to a‹
complish this through Your redeeming blood.

OUTRAGEOUS RIDICULE

Scripture reading: Luke 23:8–11

With violence it seizes my garment; it binds me about like the collar of my tunic. God has cast me into the mire, and I have become like dust and ashes.

Job 30:18, 19

Jesus was now standing before Herod. Yet He did not answer his questions. He was silent. The king felt insulted. He was extremely irritated. So he took revenge in a very low and mean way by making Jesus look ridiculous. He made Him don the white garment of a fool and laughed scornfully at His appearance.

Do we sense how much the Son of God must have suffered being made to dress in a fool's garment? Is it not much harder to be an object of laughter, than to suffer physical pain? We may be able to endure many things, but we begin to rebel when we are made to look ridiculous. When people ridicule us and destroy our dignity, it is not easy for us to forgive them.

Whom do people dare to taunt in this manner? Usually the feeble-minded, small children or animals. But ridicule can have dreadful consequences. It can inflict deep wounds and damage personalities for life.

We ridicule and humiliate others in order to exalt ourselves. So this is the sin for which Jesus had to suffer such dreadful depths of humiliation. He was willing to suffer for the depths of our sin. The rich man's craving for pleasure was punished by having his tongue burn with thirst in hell. In a similiar way we would have had to suffer sooner or later for our inflated egos—we would have been made a laughing-stock. Satan's goal is to hurl us to the depths of hell at the end of our life. There he would make us look ridiculous and show us our true selves. Through His suffering, Jesus has saved us from experiencing the terrors of hell

Our Lord has truly atoned for this sin by letting Himself be made a laughing-stock. He became the fool in our stead, so that we may again receive the share in God's glory for which we were created. Truly this is a blessing that we cannot lightly esteem. We should not frivolously cast it aside by thoughtless sarcasm and ridicule.

Jesus beneath the crown of thorns—all human dignity was taken from Him. His sore, wounded body was scantily dressed in rags. His swollen face was covered with spittle. In this nauseating condition He was led by Pilate before the yelling mob. Their faces were all distorted with rage. In His untold agony there was probably one thought that strengthened Jesus: Now that He, the image of the Father, had become abhorred by all, His people would once more be able to attain the image of God. The chastisement had fallen upon Him so that they might be redeemed.

THE MOMENT OF DECISION

Scripture reading: Mark 14:65

For it is for thy sake that I have borne reproach, that shame has covered my face. have become a stranger to my brethren, an alien to my mother's sons. For zeal for thy house has consumed me, and the insults of those who insult thee have fallen on me When I humbled my soul with fasting, i became my reproach.

Psalm 69:7-1

What a spectacle Jesus is, sitting there blindfolded, spat upon, beaten, ridiculed and mocked! This vision will be there to accuse us in heaven. We shall blush with shame

82

ecause such a thing happened on our earth. The Son of God, he holy and pure Lord, became the image of misery and we vere the ones who brought this about. We must be filled vith fear, lest we do this to our Lord again.

How often the cry, "Away with Him!" has been heard ince then. This is what we are really saying every time we sk or think, "Why should God let this happen to me?" Every ime we reject His providence for us, we are hurling our efiance at God. But for each one of us, the day will come vhen we have to decide whether we want God to reign over s or not. Because the Pharisees had not humbled themselves vhen Jesus' words and actions were hard for them to ccept, they fell into serious sin on the great day of decision. he same thing applies to us today when Jesus lays His hand pon us. If we will not humble ourselves and put aside our vishes, we are actually rebelling against God, even if we do ot realize it. We are saying, "Away with Him! We do not vant this Man to reign over us." When our great hour of emptation comes, we too will openly rebel against Him. hen in our explosive rebellion and hatefulness we will not e able to recognize ourselves.

May we often gaze upon this picture of our Lord Jesus, lasphemed and beaten, covered with blood and crowned vith a crown of thorns. It will make us want to give up the ld fortresses within us and to humble ourselves beneath the ominion of God, which is a dominion of love.

OUR FAULT!

Scripture reading: John 19:2–7

If I am wicked, woe to me! If I am righteous,
cannot lift up my head, for I am filled with
disgrace and look upon my affliction. And if
lift myself up, thou dost hunt me like a lion
and again work wonders against me; thou
dost renew thy witnesses against me, and in
crease thy vexation toward me; thou do
bring fresh hosts against me.

Job 10:15–

How could these people of long ago bear to look at Jesus s
disgraced? Why did they not open their eyes? Why did thei
hearts not cry out, "It is my fault! Stop! I am the one wh
should suffer! I deserve the crown of disgrace! My heart an
life are poisoned by the craving for recognition and atten
tion. I put on fake crowns of glory which I do not deserve
to try to gain popularity and respect in the sight of othe
men ..."? Yet no one said this to Jesus, not even His dis
ciples.

The people of long ago were carried away by the excite
ment of the moment, when they behaved in this bas
manner. Surely our actions today are far more reprehensible
For centuries now we have known the story. We can pictur
how Jesus must have looked when He was crowned wit
thorns. We can see writ large the words "for you, for you"
If we persist in retaining our crown of pride, we are de
spising Jesus once again and in a much more terrible way
By allowing men to crown Him with a crown of thorn
Jesus showed us how serious is our sin of pride. By bearin
such terrible humiliation, in our stead, He showed us ho
severe a punishment we deserve. We treat Jesus with di
dain, if we live and act as though He were never crowne
with a crown of thorns. We, His disciples, must not trea
this lightly.

AN ETERNAL STAIN

Scripture reading: Matthew 27:27–30

The Lord will judge the ends of the earth; he will give strength to his king, and exalt the power of his anointed.

1 Samuel 2:10b

Ascribe to the Lord, O families of the peoples, ascribe to the Lord glory and strength! Say among the nations, "The Lord reigns! Yea, the world is established, it shall never be moved; he will judge the peoples with equity."

Psalm 96:7, 10

O what an eternal indictment this is for us! The Son of God had to suffer such a thing—for us. We really deserve to be treated like this because of our sin! But we so lack humility that we will not humble ourselves beneath the slightest censure. We do not want to accept our true deserts. So the Son of God took the crown of thorns, for our sakes, and humbly accepted all decision, disgrace and accusations. When we look at Jesus, should we not sink down into the dust? This is where we truly belong, because of our sin. The crown of thorns will be an eternal stain upon mankind. Should we not, after this event, do everything possible to crown Jesus with a crown of glory? We often sing, "Crown Him, crown Him, Lord of all!" But how can we crown Him? We can do so by taking off our crowns and by no longer craving for a good name or reputation, position, honour and respect. If we give up all these things voluntarily, then we crown Him and award the glory to Him. When we try to be important and are concerned only with ourselves and our reputation, we are taking glory and denying it to Him.

We have been ransomed from our sins of rebellion and pride at tremendous cost. Jesus purchased our ransom with His suffering when He surrendered His divine dignity and honour and allowed Himself to be crowned with thorns. In remembrance of the humiliation and disgrace that God had to endure beneath the crown of thorns, the heavens will resound with the shout, "Glory be to the Lamb!" Even here on earth, "Glory be to the Father and to the Son and to the Holy Ghost" is heard at almost every service of worship.

Whenever we hear the word "crown", the vision of Jesus should come before our eyes. We should see the Son of God pierced and wounded by the crown of thorns. Who could then crave to wear a crown of glory? Surely we would want to cast our crown at the feet of the Lamb, that He alone might receive glory and honour. This will surely happen in heaven when those whom God created will surround His throne.

What eternal disgrace for mankind to have placed a crown of derision upon the Creator. Yet God responds to this dreadful deed by awarding crowns of glory to His faithful disciples, in His kingdom. Amazing love! No intellect can comprehend the love of God, the Father, the Son and the Holy Spirit. If only we might respond to it with an inspired desire to magnify the glory of Jesus in the sight of all men! This will happen so long as we humble ourselves beneath our sin, before God and man. By admitting that He is right when He lays His finger upon a sinful spot in our lives, we respect Jesus, the Judge upon the throne, and bring Him glory and honour.

TRUE KINGSHIP

Scripture reading: John 18:37–40; 19:1–3

But now thou hast cast off and rejected, thou art full of wrath against thy anointed. Thou hast renounced the covenant with thy servant; thou hast defiled his crown in the dust. All that pass by despoil him; he has become the scorn of his neighbours. Thou hast removed the sceptre from his hand, and cast his throne to the ground. Thou hast covered him with shame.

Psalm 89:38–39, 41, 44–45

Pilate posed the question, "So you are a king?" Jesus, beneath the crown of thorns, could only answer him by saying, "Yes, I am a King. I have come into the world to bear witness to the truth." Truly Jesus did bear witness to the truth. He mirrored us. He became what we really are: poor sinners who have deserved punishment, lowliness and death. For our sake, Jesus took the place which we deserved and thereby revealed the truth—the truth that we who have been created do not deserve thrones and crowns, but a life of humble submission. But by His example, He has also shown us that humility ennobles us. Humility merits a crown. Humility imparts royal dignity. And so Jesus shows us that man is nevertheless called to wear a crown, the crown of humility. But we may not wear this crown if, like Adam and Eve and most of mankind, we reject Him and rebel against Him. He calls us to become the Father's loving children, and to humble ourselves before the Creator, awarding Him His rightful glory. These children will one day receive crowns.

SUFFERING LOVE

Scripture reading: John 19:2–5

For this reason the Father loves me, because I lay down my life, that I may take it again. No one takes it from me, but I lay it down of my own accord.

John 10:17, 18a

Jesus said that no one could take His life from Him. He Himself was laying it down. "I give it freely." It was the free decision of His love. We see Jesus' love revealed in His voluntary abdication of His omnipotence. He let people do whatever they pleased with Him. This proves His humility. Although He had received fatal wounds from the scourging, they undressed Him and dressed Him again. How painful every movement must have been. They tortured Him in every possible way, until Pilate finally called out: "Behold the man!"

When Jesus was derided by men and crowned with a crown of thorns, He showed them how totally He could submit Himself to their rule. They had just shouted, "Away with Him! We do not want Him to impose His will on us. We do not want to be His servants!" Now Jesus showed them just how contrary was His nature to their domineering natures. Although He had created mankind, He let men subject Him to things that no one else would have meekly endured. So He demonstrated to the world for all times, that He is not a hard Master who wants to rule us. He is a Lamb, who allows others to do with Him as they will and still regards them with imploring love.

Yes, He is pure Love. He suffered torments that no other person has ever experienced. He let people ill-treat Him without resisting. In this way our Lord Jesus wanted to show us that He will never force us. He simply makes a request, "Come, follow Me. Take the way of the Lamb, of enduring love, that leads home to the Father in glory!"

THE SAME WAY

Scripture reading: Mark 15:16–19

Whoever exalts himself will be humbled and whoever humbles himself will be exalted.
Matthew 23:12

Let us now picture our Lord Jesus in our mind's eye. A holy peace lay upon the quiet Lamb. He was enduring all things in the midst of the hell that had burst out of human hearts. He would have been justified in crying out under such dreadful torture and in striking back. Yet He endured everything meekly like a lamb. He looked upon men in mercy and love. Then see what a wonderful thing happened! Everything had been taken away from Jesus—all His power and dignity. He was as lowly as a worm. (Psalm 22:6). Yet as a result of this dying to self, an eternal kingdom was born. It was entirely different from what His people had expected. It was not a kingdom of power; it was a kingdom of love!

There were some things His torturers could not take away from Him: the loving mildness of His glance, the silence of His lips. He loved and continued to love and so He was the true King and Ruler. For in the moment when His power and dominion were destroyed, His real kingship began. He was the King of all kings, the King of love.

Scripture says that we too are called to be kings, but our kingship also is related to the crown of thorns. Only those who are prepared to bear disgrace with Jesus, here on earth, will partake of His majestic glory in heaven, at the throne of God. "If we endure, we shall also reign with him." (2 Timothy 2:12). To the extent that His disciples become humble, His kingdom of love will be able to grow. This growth does not result from much work or through the power of our gifts and personality. This kingdom is built only upon a broken and contrite heart.

Our Lord Jesus suffered beneath the crown of thorns. He was tortured and His strength was broken, but He still loved His enemies. This is the guarantee that the divine Kingdom of love will come into being. The greatest suffering or Satanic attack cannot destroy this kingdom, because what is built by love is eternal and indestructible. The little flock which belongs to this kingdom follows Jesus along the way of the Lamb. They humble themselves before God and man. They demonstrate to the world what Jesus, the King of this kingdom, is like. He is the King of love. One day they will inherit His kingdom with Him.

Just as the wonderful perfume of precious ointment filled the air when the vessel was broken, so the glory and beauty of Jesus became apparent when He was ridiculed and crowned with thorns. Indeed, the perfume of love flowed forth from the tortured Lamb of God. Jesus was wonderfully majestic in His lowliness. He was overflowing with love in the face of mockery and rejection. His love and mercy reveal our rebellion more clearly than could any court of justice. This portrait of Jesus has power to overcome our sin. It will conquer our pride and rebellion. It will remould us in the image of God, in the image of love and humility.

O Jesus, You shall ever be adored.

You allowed Your holy countenance to be utterly disfigured so that our faces might reflect Your great beauty. Truly You have won the majesty of the divine image for us. We can reflect Your image. One day we will shine like suns in Your kingdom and enter the presence of the Father.

O sight demanding silence,
In heaven all bow to reverence
The Lamb with crown of thorns.
Adoring angels gazing
Upon this sight amazing,
Perplexed can never understand.

This sight such grief exposing,
The love of God disclosing,
Of Father, Spirit, Son.
Beyond man's art expressing
Pain radiant with such blessing,
Christ's countenance of loving grace.

It beams with love's clear splendour,
With patience strong and tender
Beneath that crown of thorns;
To master all men's scheming,
The cursing and blaspheming,
With power to heal and reconcile.

W.J. 65

ord Jesus,
I worship Your countenance so beautiful and majestic.
he heavens reflect Your glory. Hosts of cherubim are ab-
orbed in adoration of Your face. Its holy light heals man-
ind. I worship Your holy countenance, the most beautiful
ver seen on earth. You should have been crowned with
ajestic crowns of power and glory—but You became the
ymbol of dishonour and agony. You were so disfigured that
eople hid their faces from You.
Lord Jesus, I worship You in the beauty of Your suffering.
the midst of torture and pain, You were still radiant with
ve and mercy. Disfigured by our wickedness, beaten and
at upon, You still gazed with mercy upon those who
ocked and ill-treated You.

Holy Spirit,
You have shown me how despised Jesus was, although all
eatures on earth should love and honour Him for His
ory, love and beauty. I entreat You to fill me with ardent

love for Jesus, so that I no longer seek glory for myself but always honour Him above all and bring Him glory. From now on let me show my gratitude to Jesus for all His suffering beneath the crown of thorns, by offering Him such love.

Christ crowned with thorns adoring,
Love watches Him enduring
Men's ridicule and scorn.
Love praises Him who suffered,
To whom they insults offered,
Praises His love 'neath crown of thorns.

Their praises are unending,
In triumph loud ascending,
They pierce through hell's grim walls.
As once He was derided,
So now the Lamb is lauded,
For ever now as Victor hailed.

I worship You, O Jesus,

and Your marvellous love, which endured ridicule, blasphemy and agony for the sake of us sinners. You have restored our lost dignity to us. You have granted us the right to live as citizens and members of God's family in the heavenly kingdom. How can I ever thank You enough for removing the angel with a sword who stood before the gates of the holy city of God to deny me entrance?

I worship You, O Father,

and Your wonderful love. You laid Your own honour in the dust. You permitted Your only Son, the Most High, to become the most despised of all men. You let His holy name be blasphemed.

I thank You for allowing this to happen solely for us, so that we might regain the honour we lost. You wanted to give us another chance to become kings and priests. One day we will join with all the angels in adoration at the throne of the Lamb.

King with many crowns now crowned,
Lord o'er many lords enthroned,
Now majestic reigning.
Heaven its homage to You pays,
Blood-bought sinners sing Your praise,
Worship You for ever.

CARRYING THE CROSS

As they led Him away, they seized one Simon of Cyrene, who was coming in from the country, and laid on him the cross, to carry it behind Jesus. And there followed him a great multitude of the people, and of women who bewailed and lamented him. But Jesus turning to them said, "Daughters of Jerusalem, do not weep for me, but weep for yourselves and for your children. For behold, the days are coming when they will say, 'Blessed are the barren, and the wombs that never bore, and the breasts that never gave suck!' Then they will begin to say to the mountains, 'Fall on us'; and to the hills, 'Cover us.' For if they do this when the wood is green, what will happen when it is dry?" Two others also, who were criminals, were led away to be put to death with him.

Luke 23:26–32

A wooden cross is swinging low
Down from the highest throne.
To Christ, the Son of God 'twill go,
To Him, to Him alone.

He bends down low beneath that cross,
Though He's Creator God.
He made the whole wide universe,
But earth rejects its Lord.

A cross outlined against the sky.
For sin Christ will atone.
The Holy One is lifted high,
To win for us a throne.

THE VICTORIOUS CROSS

Scripture reading: John 19:14–17

For the word of the cross is folly to those who
are perishing, but to us who are being saved it
is the power of God.

1 Corinthians 1:1

They laid the cross upon Jesus.

How hell must have raged! Jesus had become, so to speak,
wedded to the cross. It had become the symbol of redemption. Jesus and the cross had become one. Every step He
took, the cross went with Him. He had become the cross-
bearer. Soon He would be the crucified Lord. To the end of
time Jesus will be pictured on the cross. In this way He is
known and loved—and also hated. The cross has become an
eternal symbol, the symbol of redemption, the symbol of
victory over hell. Jesus knew this and this is why He carried
His cross.

Is there anyone who does not long to share His victory
today and to be one of His chosen ones when He makes His
triumphant entry into the world? Who would not want to
have fellowship in suffering with Him who brought the
cross and can never be separated from it? Is there anyone
who does not want to be the beloved of the Father? Surely
He must have looked down with great love upon His Son
when He carried His cross. We also are beloved by Him
when He sees that we carry our cross out of love for Jesus.

Come follow Me,
My Simon be,
Come follow Me.

But who for Him a cross will bear?
He seeks for one who longs His way to share.

O hear His plea,
Come follow Me,
My Simon be.

O where, O where can even one be found
Who, out of love for Christ, to cross is bound?

In glory he
Enthroned shall be
And Jesus see.

Jesus said, "Where I am, there shall my servant be also." John 12:26). Because He loves His disciples so much, He has promised to share everything with them. He wants to draw us into the fellowship of His sufferings so that we may bring forth much fruit with Him. Streams of life will pour forth from people who take Jesus' yoke and bear their suffering out of love for Him. Thousands can be blessed by one person who follows Jesus, and carries his cross. What an opportunity! Is there anyone who would choose to miss it, by ignoring Jesus' request, "Take my yoke upon you"? (Matthew 11:29).

AN EASY YOKE

Scripture reading: Matthew 27:31, 32

Take my yoke upon you and learn from me; for I am gentle and lowly in heart, and you will find rest for your souls. For my yoke is easy and my burden is light.
Matthew 11:29, 30

Humble people accept the burdens that others put upon them and still think life is better than they deserve. The proud, however, make many demands and always believe they have the right to good things. Only because Jesus was "lowly in heart" could He say, "Yea Father, yea most willingly I'll bear what Thou commandest." Because He was so humble He could take up His cross and bear the guilt of others.

But we do not want to bear even our own guilt. If we had a humble, contrite heart, we would be willing to bear the consequences of our sin. Even the worst sufferings that came upon us would seem light compared with what we reckoned we deserved for our sin. If we have a contrite heart, the hardest chastening and the heaviest crosses would seem small in comparison to our great sin. We would no longer be surprised by the sins of others. We would not react against them and criticise them. We would humble ourselves, knowing that we stand under the same condemnation. If we were really truthful and humble, we would have to admit: As I am now, I could not possibly reach the glory of God. I thank You, my Father, for Your great love in chastening me. know You give me crosses to bear only so that I may share Your holiness (Hebrews 12:10).

From the very beginning God has declared that His yoke is easy and His burden light. (Matthew 11:30). But in our pride we think we know better. We think that the burden God has laid upon us is too heavy. Therefore, we do not take it up and carry it. We keep weighing it in our hands to see how heavy it is. If we do this, it really does become heavier and heavier until finally it is too heavy to bear.

If we truly see our sin, we will react to our crosses as loving children of the dearest Father. We will join with Jesus, our Brother and Bridegroom saying, "Yea Father, yea most willingly I'll bear what Thou commandest." When we say "Yes" in this way the heavens will open and pour grace into our hearts. We will be strengthened to bear our grief. We will have to confess, "Your yoke is easy and the fruit of Your suffering is sweet. This is entirely true."

DELAYED SO LONG

Scripture reading: John 19:16, 17

A man had a fig tree planted in his vineyard; and he came seeking fruit on it and found none.

Luke 13:6

How very few have won the glory that lies hidden in the cross!

The Father looks down from heaven sadly and asks, 'Where are those who have experienced the blessings of suffering? Who has been comforted in suffering? Where are those truly redeemed, who do not live in bondage to their suffering? Where are those who in the midst of darkness can rejoice that they have been redeemed?" Jesus probably has to lament, "There are very few. Yet, I suffered bitterly to redeem them. I drank the cup of suffering unto death for them, so that suffering would no longer lead to death, but to a new and blessed life. But who cares about My suffering? Your small troubles would seem trivial, if you saw My grief! I offer you the fruit of My suffering: Resurrection. A new and blessed life—divine life.''

When we suffer, do we ever think of Jesus' suffering? All the suffering of the world is contained in His suffering. If we were to spend all our time thinking about our own troubles and spared just one thought for His suffering, we would see His amazing love. Lovingly He suffered for our sakes, to heal our wounds and to comfort our hearts. If we really grasped this fact, we would be full of joy.

My Lord Jesus,

You show us clearly that crosses bring both suffering and glory. It was Your cross that brought us glory. The crosses

99

You allow us to bear will also bring us glory, if we carry them with You. So let me think of my cross with You in mind. Then I shall praise You for the transformation and glory that it will bring me. I thank You for giving me strength to carry my cross in such a way that it will bring You glory and much fruit.

Through Jesus, the cross has become a source of life. Because we do not embrace our crosses lovingly, there are few streams of life flowing from us to bring life and blessing to others. When we bear our cross and die to our self, new life is born. There is no other way to bring life. When we shake off our cross, we are like the dead who can no longer give birth to life. We are no longer in the stream of life, but are at rest in a sepulchre.

If we love Jesus, we will also love our cross. Then we will receive abundant life.

My Lord Jesus,

Let me come today into the light of truth. Show me how often I have rejected or thrown away the cross that You sent me. When I could not escape from it, I bore it unwillingly and grudgingly. Help me repent now that I have heard Your voice and seen the grief I have caused You. Do not let my heart be hardened. I entreat Your Holy Spirit to grant me tears of true repentance, to free me from my desire to escape the cross.

I claim the Bible promise, God "calls into existence the things that do not exist." (Romans 4:17). You will give me what I lack—love for my cross. You have overcome my unwillingness to carry a cross by bearing it Yourself and by dying for me.

LOWLY IN HEART

Scripture reading: Mark 15:20–22

Behold my servant, whom I uphold, my chosen, in whom my soul delights; I have put my Spirit upon him, he will bring forth justice to the nations. He will not cry or lift up his voice, or make it heard in the street.

Isaiah 42:1, 2

Jesus was bowed lower and lower under His cross. Finally He fell in the dust. This is where our crosses are designed to bring us also. God sends us a cross of suffering so that our proud hearts will be humbled in the dust. But usually we resist and shake off our cross.

Jesus, however, took up the cross. He is the only one who did not need the burden of the cross to teach Him to humble Himself. He was truly the humblest of all. He took up the cross for us, because we will not humble ourselves beneath God's powerful hand. Jesus must often have felt the loving clasp of His Father's hand while He was with Him in His kingdom. He experienced His invisible blessing of love, on earth, when God the Father spoke to Him from time to time, "This is my beloved Son with whom I am well pleased." But now the hand of God came upon Him in a different way. It was like the hand of a stranger—hard and heavy—like the hand of an enemy. But even worse, it was as though this "enemy" had conquered Him and was pressing Him down, with his foot, saying. "You are doomed!"

The burden that was laid upon Jesus was so heavy that it brought Him to death. But from then onwards the cross has become a tree of life and blessing for all who will carry it with Him. The cross, which has truly become the tree of life, bears wonderful fruit. The burden of the cross transforms men into new creatures, fit to inherit heavenly life. We become new people, if we bear our crosses humbly. The old, evil nature dies and we are transformed into the image of Jesus, the patient, humble, loving Lamb. So, if you seek true happiness, do not try to escape the cross any more, for joy is hidden in it.

So I Your cross praise constantly,
In it Your loving purpose see;
I will extol its power to bring
Much fruit of grace from suffering.

This cross Your children humbles so,
As we beneath its load bend low,
That heaven's door is opened wide,
And we are set God's Son beside.

W.J. 71

Lord Jesus,

Through Your example You have taught me to humble myself low beneath the cross. You had to humble Yourself under the hand of God, because we always fail to do so. You are lowly in heart, so You bowed down in the dust under the burden of the cross, instead of throwing it off. I ask You to help me to humble myself too when You lay a cross upon me, for I am a sinner who deserves to carry burdens.

Although I deserve to lie in the dust, I would never do so willingly. Please let my cross bring me to this point. O God, You are the Holy One, yet You humble Yourself, but I, a sinner, refuse to do so. Please do not let me continue like this any longer. Grant that I may be ashamed to see You still carrying the cross for me, because I have refused to humble myself beneath it.

DEPRIVED OF HIS DIVINE POWER

Scripture reading: Luke 23:26–32

Turn to me and take pity on me; give thy strength to thy servant, and save the son of thy handmaid.

Psalm 86:16

From the manner in which Jesus bore the burden of His cross, we can see His humility and the dedication of His will. He did not bear it as a great martyr, nor with power and might. No, He bore it with human weakness. For this reason He fell under the weight of the cross and was humiliated in the eyes of man. He did not convert it into a heroic deed. Deprived of all divine power, He bore the cross in great weakness and with complete willingness so that the radiance of His humility and His humanity would become wonderfully manifest.

His fall reveals even more of His humility. People claim that He did not really bear our burden. They take away His glory. Any shred that was left, He shared with another man, who helped Him bear the cross. That is how poor and lowly Jesus became when He bore the cross.

The way of such lowliness, however, leads to the throne. The Lord Jesus, with His wounds still visible, is seated upon the throne. He is surrounded by those who followed Him in humility, bearing their cross! Who would not praise the cross? In the cross we meet Jesus. Not only in the cross of Calvary, but also in every cross we have to bear. Let us join in the exultant cry of the Apostle Paul, "We rejoice in our sufferings!" (Romans 5:3).

OUT OF LOVE FOR US

Scripture reading: John 19:16, 17

The Lord has laid on him the iniquity of us all.

Isaiah 53:6

Jesus embraced His cross in love and carried it, because He wanted to redeem us. Let this show us how eternally He embraces us in love, burdened with sin as we are. After all He was so weakened He could have avoided carrying the cross at all. But no, Jesus struggled on with it as long as He possibly could. He embraced us with our burden of sin in order to put our sin to death on the cross.

If we doubt whether our Lord Jesus loves us, we need only to visualize Him carrying the cross. He carried our burden to the very end—not because He was obliged to do so, but in love and humility. Truly on His body He carried all the burdens of sin to the cross. Let us not do Jesus any further hurt by imagining we cannot cope with our burden of sin—that we have to bear it alone. He has taken it upon Himself—the whole weight of it! We can be made whole because our chastisement was laid upon Him.

If we believe this we will reckon with what Jesus did for us and not with what we can do. It means facing our heavy burden of sin and saying, ". . . the Lord has laid on him the iniquity of us all." (Isaiah 53:6).

O depths of loving mercy sweet,
For us You bore this pain so deep,
For us, for us poor sinners.
Beneath the cross we humbly fall,
Adore the Lamb who saved us all,
Our grievous sins bewailing.

W.J. 72.

SPECTATOR OR FOLLOWER?

Scripture reading: Luke 23:26–28

If any man would come after me, let him deny himself and take up his cross daily and follow me. For whoever would save his life will lose it; and whoever loses his life for my sake, he will save it.

Luke 9:23, 24

Today too Jesus is asking us to carry the cross with Him—not under compulsion like Simon of Cyrene, but of our own free will, out of love. "Whoever wants to follow Me must take up his cross daily." Consequently, Jesus does not say, "If you are humbled and humiliated, submit and you will be exalted." No, He says, "Whoever humbles himself will be exalted." (Matthew 23:12). Jesus does not say, "Let people put a cross upon you", but rather, "Whoever takes up his cross . . .!" He is seeking people who will take up the cross of their own free will, not ones, like Simon, who accept burdens which are imposed upon them. He seeks people who are willing to seize opportunities to become lowly. This is the way of love. These are the only ones whom Jesus calls "disciples". He says, "He who does not take his cross and follow me is not worthy of me."

Are there not many more spectators than true followers among Christians? There is one thing we lack: love which voluntarily serves others. Spectators run alongside for a while, like the people who watched Jesus carrying His cross. They know about His sufferings and perhaps even feel sorry for Him, yet on the whole they remain spectators. The true followers, however, out of love for Jesus, follow in His footsteps and carry their cross. For love has to be with the loved one. It must be at His side. It must partake of His way of endurance, of suffering, of disgrace, of lowliness and forsakenness. It treads where Jesus trod. And behold, the most difficult way then becomes easy. Love changes everything. It transforms sorrow into joy.

O listen all, His heart will break,
The whole world's cross He still must take,
For no one else will bear it.
Today He suffers grief and pain,
He suffers loneliness again,
When we refuse our crosses.

Jesus has taken the sting out of our cross and so it is our own fault if we cannot cope with it. If we feel oppressed by it, it is probably because we are blaming God and other people when problems arise, instead of ourselves. Through our pride we have created a wall between God and ourselves. We have locked God out and so the blessing, peace, comfort and glory which the cross was meant to bring, cannot flow into our hearts.

When the cross was cast at Jesus' feet, the act implied "You are fit only to carry our burdens—You are our servant, the servant of all!" Jesus shouldered it as though this was what He deserved. Like a brother, He joined our ranks. Indeed He even made Himself inferior to us. We have never found another servant willing to bear all our burdens. This is abundantly clear in our times, when no one wants to take up anyone else's burdens and become a servant.

No one could be found anywhere to take up the infinitely heavy burden of sin—the masses of sins of all mankind. Who could have carried it? But the burdens were there. Only Jesus was willing to be the One "good enough for such a job". At last mankind had Someone upon whom they could unload anything and everything. Jesus was there, the Servant of all.

Lord, through Zion's streets so narrow,
Staggering 'neath the weighty cross,
Deeply to that cross committed
Saving man at bitter cost,

Steadily You still go onward
To Your goal, Mount Golgotha,
Where You give Yourself as Victim
On the cross they lifted there.

W.J. 69

Lord Jesus,

We worship You for patiently bearing the burdens of the world upon Your back, meekly as a lamb. We worship You for every bitter step You trod along the way of the cross. You stooped deeply beneath its burden, out of love for us, so that our feet may now tread the path to the city of God.

We worship You, O Jesus. Although You sit upon the highest throne, surrounded by cherubim, You let Yourself be laid in the dust, because of our pride. We sinners do not want to humble ourselves beneath God's powerful hand. We do not want to lie in the dust, so You filled this place for us.

Jesus bears the heavy cross beam
To the hill of Golgotha.
Here we see such pain and suffering
That outstrips man's reasoning far.
For 'tis God who bears that cross beam
Which to criminals belongs,
Yet no voice for Him was pleading
From amongst those jostling throngs.

Jesus, You, the burden-bearer,
Stand now in the sinners' place,
In Your mercy for us sinners
Man's dilemma You embrace.
But You still must bear our crosses
For we push them all away,
Yet You bore Your cross that henceforth
We might conquer ours each day.

W.J. 69

My Lord Jesus,

I thank You for carrying the cross. It gives me a glimpse into Your heart, and I see how great was Your willingness to suffer. Before the foundation of the world You chose the cross. You wanted to bear the cross. You wanted to suffer. How greatly You must have loved us! And how much You must love us today, because You still choose the sorrow and pain which we usually try to avoid.

I worship You, for You need not have chosen to suffer. You are almighty, You could have spoken one word and transformed Your sorrow into joy. But You chose to suffer out of love for us.

I worship You, Jesus. While You were on earth You healed the sick, You freed those who were possessed by devils. You raised people from the dead. You were truly a messenger of joy wherever You went. You ventured into night and death to bring us joy. In all Your great distress, You did not evoke Your divine power in so much as a single word to lighten Your cross. Instead You suffered to the utmost the most dreadful agony that man has ever borne, to free us from the curse of suffering. I worship Your marvellous love.

Should I now not praise You, the Cross-bearer, and take up my cross and follow You?

You bear the cross, O Jesus,
Our King and Lord of power,
Deprived of strength and honour
For this is evil's hour.

You stoop beneath its burden,
Along the crowded road;
For us, for love of sinners,
You bear this heavy load.

You, Lord, were always ready
To help and heal and bless;

Yet when Your strength is failing,
None aid in Your distress.

O let me be Your Simon,
For this myself I give,
To share Your cross's burden,
In love for You to live.

W.J. 70

Lord Jesus,

I entreat You, let me join those who bear their cross willingly and happily and so become Your cross-bearers. I ask
You to incorporate me into the host of cross-bearers who
belong to You, the Cross-bearer. Let me be willing to follow
You, with them, along Your way of the cross and so come
into Your intimate presence and fellowship. I should like to
be where You are—here on earth, with You on Your way of
the cross—and above, with You in glory. Answer my prayer
and let my love for You increase daily so that my love for
the cross may also increase.

O Son of God, be praised and blessed!
You came to us at love's behest
To tread the way of suffering.
O cross of hidden glory bright,
Radiant with heavenly joy and light,
Who could not help but praise You!
Who could not help but praise You!

We, the redeemed, should love the cross;
You did not let its pain and loss
Hinder You, sweet Lord Jesus.
Henceforth beneath the cross I'll fight,
My standard now, my crown to be,
Yes, bound to it forever,
Yes, bound to it forever.

Lord Jesus,

I worship You. Through carrying the cross and through Your crucifixion, You have redeemed me from my fear of the cross. You have shown me that salvation is hidden in the cross and You have made me long to love it. When You hung on the cross and cried out, "It is finished!", You put all fear of suffering to death. You won for all those who believe in Your victory the ability to love their cross. You have given us access to the precious things hidden in the cross and let us share in the glory that it brings. With all my heart I thank You for this.

Cross of love and cross of suffering,
Cross of wondrous glory bright,
Cross of weeping, richest harvest
Sown with tears in darkest night.

Cross of wonder brightly gleaming
Like a thousand suns doth shine,
Cross of Jesus, Lord most holy,
Giver of its light divine.

Cross of Jesus, whom we honour,
We will love His cross so bright,
Cross of love, O purge our motives,
Purify them in Your light.

Cross of love, let all our motives
Now be bound to Jesu's love,
This the sign that shows us plainly
How we mount to heaven above.

Cross that urges, draws and leads us
Up to heaven's highest throne,
There to live with Christ for ever,
All for One, for One alone.

W.J. 214

Love compelled Jesus to carry His cross to Calvary and to die there, on the cross, for the redemption of the world. His mind was absolutely set on this. Jesus had come to earth to die. The Apostle Paul had the mind of Christ, when he wrote, "To die is gain." (Philippians 1:21). Death brings gain for many souls. Because Jesus had this powerful love for the cross, it will be carried like a flame in the hearts of all His disciples who have His Spirit in them. "Anyone who does not have the Spirit of Christ does not belong to him," said the Apostle (Romans 8:9). Love for the cross should be a characteristic feature of the disciples of Jesus. It should make them recognizable as His disciples.

Cross-bearing—blessèd pain,
Glory its final gain,
Loaded with gold is the cross,
Bringing grace all its own
From heaven's highest throne,
Cross-bearing brings us bliss.

Bearing the cross of Christ,
Who can such grace assess?
Drawing me close to my Lord.
Sharing with Him the weight;
Truly an honour great,
Yielding eternal bliss!

W.J. 211

THE CRUCIFIXION

And when they came to a place called Golgotha (which means the place of a skull), they offered him wine to drink, mingled with gall; but when he tasted it, he would not drink it. And when they had crucified him, they divided his garments among them by casting lots; then they sat down and kept watch over him there. And over his head they put the charge against him, which read, "This is Jesus the King of the Jews." Then two robbers were crucified with him, one on the right and one on the left. And those who passed by derided him, wagging their heads and saying, "You who would destroy the temple and build it in three days, save yourself! If you are the Son of God, come down from the cross." So also the chief priests, with the scribes and elders, mocked him, saying, "He saved others; he cannot save himself. He is the King of Israel; let him come down now from the cross, and we will believe in him. He trusts in God; let God deliver him now, if he desires him; for he said, 'I am the Son of God'." And the robbers who were crucified with him also reviled him in the same way.

Now from the sixth hour there was darkness over all the land until the ninth hour. And about the ninth hour Jesus cried with a loud voice, "Eli, Eli, lama sabachthani?" that is, "My God, my God, why hast thou forsaken me?" And some of the bystanders hearing it said, "This man is calling Elijah." And one of them at once ran and took a sponge, filled it with vinegar, and put it on a reed, and gave it to him to drink. But the others said, "Wait, let us see whether Elijah will come to save him." And Jesus cried again with a loud voice and yielded up his spirit.

And behold, the curtain of the temple was torn in two, from top to bottom; and the earth shook, and the rocks were split; the tombs also were opened, and many bodies of the saints who had fallen asleep were raised, and coming out of the tombs after his resurrection they went into the holy city and appeared to many. When the centurion and those who were with him, keeping watch over Jesus, saw the earthquake and what took place, they were filled with awe, and said, "Truly this was the Son of God!"

There were also many women there, looking on from afar, who had followed Jesus from Galilee, ministering to him; among whom were Mary Magdalene, and Mary the mother of James and Joseph and the mother of the sons of Zebedee.

Matthew 27:33–56

To death our God is going,
O earth, be silent now.
The angel hosts adore Him,
Before His feet they bow.
Awake mankind, behold Him,
Your Maker on the cross!
For you, for you, ye sinners,
He darkness chose and loss.

Awake, creation, groaning
In woe and misery!
To bring about redemption
Your Maker dies for thee.
O let the whole world humbly
Before Him prostrate fall;
Let every creature praise Him,
Who stripped Himself of all.

Praised be that holy day in the midst of the ages, when You, the Son of God, went forth to die.

Praised be that holy hour, when heaven became silent and the angels veiled their faces—the earth shook and creatures moaned.

Praised be the hour of Your death, when You, the very essence of life, the Creator of all things, became a captive of death to bring us sinners eternal life.

THE CRUEL HAMMER

Scripture reading: Luke 23:33-35

They have pierced my hands and feet.

Psalm 22:16b

The Son of God was laid upon the cross. He had clung faith-
fully to the cross until the end of the journey. But then He
was to become one with the cross. He was to be nailed to it.
He was to die upon it. New instruments of torture came in
view. In addition to the chains of the arrest, the whips of the
scourging and the crown of thorns, we can now see the huge
nails and the hammer.

How Jesus must have trembled when He saw them! What
grief must have pierced the Father's heart as the time for this
cruel, new torture approached His Son. Nailed to the cross!
When we talk of nailing things, we usually mean lifeless
objects. We hammer nails through them, but they are insen-
sitive. We do not work on living creatures with hammers
and nails. But the Son of Man, who is the Son of God, the
Creator of man, was less respected and worse treated than a
lifeless object. With crude violence they hammered nails
into His hands and feet. Those hands created and sustained
the world. One day, all His enemies, together with the whole
universe, will fall down at those feet.

But it had to happen. The hands and feet of the Son of God
had to be pierced so that His redeeming blood could flow for
the salvation of a lost world. Only through wounds could
salvation flow forth. How would those bleeding wounds
have been made if there had been no hammer or nails? Jesus,
the Lamb that was slain, is marked with the wounds made
by the nails. Seated on His throne, He bears them still, be-

cause they are the symbol of the salvation He brought to mankind. That is why God the Father could not hold back the hammer. This instrument would bring such great salvation to the whole world. His heart was overflowing with merciful love for His children. He desired to give them the blood of redemption to drink, from His Son's wounds, no matter what it cost Him.

Whoever wants to let others drink of his blood must allow himself to be wounded. So before the foundation of the world, the Father, the Son and the Holy Spirit, committed themselves to this cruel act of being nailed to the cursed tree. It cost the Son of God His life, because the wounds were fatal, but they still bring life to mankind. God's very essence was poured out through Jesus' wounds and all who acknowledge His blood in faith will partake of the divine nature and be redeemed by His love.

We worship and adore You, O Lord, for Your untold suffering in the hour of death. Your arms and legs were stretched so tight, causing You incomprehensible pain. This is an eternal symbol of Your love stretching out far to us sinners, to bring us home to the Father's heart.

We worship and adore Your loving heart. It was broken by suffering at the ninth hour. But from then onwards, eternal redemption has flowed from it to all sinners.

We worship and adore You, for amidst all the torture You had only one great thirst. Your love thirsted for lost sinners, for those whom You had created. This caused Your holy cry, "I thirst!" (John 19:28).

We praise You, O Jesus, Son of God, for at the point of death You proclaimed Your victory with the most powerful cry: "It is finished!"

LOVE BORE OUR CURSE

Scripture reading: Mark 15:27–28

Christ redeemed us from the curse of the law, having become a curse for us—for it is written, "Cursed be every one who hangs on a tree".

Galatians 3:13

Jesus hung on the tree and so, according to the law, He became accursed. All the curses that would otherwise have lain upon sinners, upon criminals, lay upon Him, for He bore our sin. Yes, He was made sin. Therefore, according to the law, the curse of God must strike Him. Those upon whom the curse actually lay, could now become absolutely free. The law was completely fulfilled. The curse that should have fallen on us sinners has been removed for ever. It did not fall on our bodies, but on His body.

In place of this curse, we sinners have received the blessings of the love and grace of God. He has accepted us as His beloved children. We, the godless, who should have been cursed and condemned to hell, are made righteous, so that we can enter the kingdom of divine love and glory. Jesus won the mantle of righteousness for us, when He became cursed in our stead. How wonderful is His love!

Calvary! In heaven and on earth there can be only one anthem of praise—the great anthem of God's love. Love died for us. Love was crucified to set free a thief and bring him to Paradise. Love opened the gates of hell and rescued His children from the hands of death. This love will not rest until it has drawn everyone to the Father's home.

WE HAD NO PART?

Scripture reading: Luke 23:39–43

If thou, O Lord, shouldst mark iniquities, Lord,
who could stand? But there is forgiveness with
thee, that thou mayest be feared.

Psalm 130:3, 4

When we look at Jesus suffering on the cross, none of us
may say we bear no guilt for His death. All of us have
helped to torture Him to death. The sins of the whole world
came together at His crucifixion—my sin is there also. My
sin put Him to death. His crucifixion finds us all guilty of sin.
We must accept this indictment and sink down at the foot
of the cross, owning our guilt. Only then can we partake of
the redemption that Jesus won when He bore all our sins to
the cross.

Each one of us, therefore, must heed these words: Recognize yourself in all the events that led to Jesus' death. We
must acknowledge our own sin in this terrible scene of torture. Every time we are chastened and have to follow a path
that is hard for us, let us say, "I am paid according to my
deeds. I declare myself guilty." Then Jesus will answer,
"Today you will be with me in Paradise." (Luke 23:43).

Fastening our attention on His crucifixion, let us pray that
the Holy Spirit may shed light on our sin—the sin that
brought Jesus to the cross. Then we can be granted forgiveness.

O sight of grief amazing,
A cross is lifted high;
Bowed low, the heavens are gazing
For soon their God will die.
O tremble now each sinner,
Repent, yourself abase,

There hangs your Lord and Maker,
So full of love and grace.

O merciful decision
Of God to go to death,
To bring men to contrition
And save this sin-sick earth.
O ne'er such grief and suffering
Was seen in earth or heaven;
The Father's precious offering,
The Lamb, to cross is given.

O sinners mourn, lamenting,
You cause Him so much pain;
Go, tell all men, repenting,
Your sins have Jesus slain.
Despised and mocked and hated,
For your sake, yours alone,
His life He dedicated
To win for you a crown.

THE REJECTED SACRIFICE

Scripture reading: Mark 15:29–32

Is it nothing to you, all you who pass by
Look and see if there is any sorrow like my
sorrow which was brought upon me, which
the Lord inflicted on the day of his fierce
anger.

Lamentations 1:12

Death is darkness, loneliness, separation. It is the end of all
things here on earth. For Jesus death meant separation from
His people. He had come amongst them from another world
and had spent thirty-three years with them. What was this

parting like? His chosen people shed no tears for Him. No one, except those closest to Him, felt the least regret that this most precious Guest from another world was being parted from them by death. On the contrary, His parting was accompanied by scornful voices shouting, "Help Yourself!" These were His chosen people's final words to Him.

In such a manner the Son of God passed from His life amongst men. It must have been a dark night for His soul. He had poured out His love like a stream upon His children. In the hour of death, the soul is most sensitive. It seeks for a word, a token of love. It hungers for love in this hour. But Jesus was answered with hatred—hatred that put Him to death. Yet Jesus' love could not be stifled, for it is stronger than the hatred of hell. Hell was forced to discover that the power of love is invincible. Love could be attacked, betrayed, forsaken and disappointed. Love could be hated, ridiculed, slandered and scorned. Love could be sentenced to death and made to bear a heavy cross. Love was assaulted by all these enemies, but it was stronger than all of them. Jesus' love took them captive. The more they beat Him, the more glorious and victorious was the radiance of His love.

Hell was made to discover that in the hour that love is put to death, it rises again triumphantly to life. For love is true life, divine life. It can never be killed, either in Jesus, its Head, or in His members.

Who can understand this mystery? Jesus is eternal Love. He will always live, for He is the life of all. Yet He was despised, mocked, tortured and put to death. But in dying, love will always rise again. Truly in the very manner of dying, love gains such power that sinners break down at the foot of the cross. They are conquered by crucified Love, and so become messengers of love.

Lord Jesus,
On the cross You became the true image of love, all-inclusive love. Love embraces enemies as well as friends. Love

is stronger than death and hell. In death, love proved its great power.

You have redeemed me to perfect love and to nothing less than this. So in view of Your cross, I will dedicate myself to You, O eternal Love. I will dedicate myself to love with an all-embracing love. I will love my neighbours and strangers, my enemies as well as my friends, the members of my own church and those of other denominations. I will dedicate myself to a love that excludes no one—a love that never ceases. I know that You will give me this love, the love that flows from Your heart.

THE VEIL WAS TORN

Scripture reading: Matthew 27:46–52

My God, my God, why hast thou forsaken me? Why art thou so far from helping me, from the words of my groaning? Yet thou art holy enthroned on the praises of Israel.

Psalm 22:1, 3

For our sake, for us sinners, Jesus had to experience what it is like to be forsaken by the Father. There was no other way in which we could be allowed to return to the fellowship of the Father, in Paradise. Who can say whose grief was the greater—the Father's or the Son's? It was one grief, because the Father and the Son are one. Even though they were separated, they continued to suffer together. The Father had to cut Himself off from the Son; He had to veil Himself as though He had forsaken Him. He had to stand by and watch His Son suffering the torment of being forsaken. And the Son, enduring this awful separation from God, no longer understood the Father.

It was indeed dark night, a night of hellish torture, for God was separated from God. Heaven had always worshipped the Godhead as a Trinity. How it must have shuddered at this suffering! But while God the Father and God the Son were parted in this way, the curtain in the Temple was rent—the union between God and man had been achieved.

I adore You, Lord Jesus. I worship Your amazing love. For us You bore the Father's wrath. We would otherwise have been separated from Him eternally and delivered to the prince of hell and the everlasting fire. Truly, You suffered the torment of hell upon the cross so that we might escape hell for eternity.

I adore You. I worship the love that tasted such bitter death for our sake so that we might taste divine life in Your kingdom for eternity.

I adore You, and worship Your amazing love. For our sake You wanted to bear this hour of desolation, this hour filled with the most fearful torment. You suffered so that we would not have to be separated from the Father's love for a single moment, either in this world or in eternity.

THE HEART OF LOVE WAS PIERCED

Scripture reading: John 19:33–37

Love bears all things, believes all things, hopes all things, endures all things. Love never ends.

1 Corinthians 13:7, 8

When Jesus was dead, His heart was pierced by a spear and blood flowed forth. His precious gift of salvation poured forth from this wound; likewise up to the very point of death precious gifts of blessing poured forth from His wounded soul. He spoke only words of love and mercy. "Father, forgive them!" "Today you will be with me in Paradise." "This is your son! This is your mother!"

O what a heart was broken here! Even in eternity we shall never fully comprehend the depths of His merciful love. The more painfully His heart was wounded, tortured and torn to shreds, the more love and mercy flowed out of it—never any bitterness. Surely there was an awestruck silence in heaven when Jesus spoke these words in the hour when He was so deeply wounded and disappointed. No doubt the angels bowed before their Creator, weeping. They would be overwhelmed by such powerful love in the midst of the unimaginable horror of this hour of death. The Father's heart must have been filled with pain, for the suffering of His Child. Can we not imagine His saying, with even more love than ever before, "This is my beloved Son, with whom I am well pleased."?

Love bled to death in order to flow forth from a thousand wounds into a world full of hatred and death. It flows to transform and redeem people from hatred to love.

O Jesus Christ, the Life of all mankind,
You lie here dead, that death for us be changed.
O love beyond comparing!
Yes, love beyond comparing!
The bitter pangs of death, the grave You chose
And from Your bleeding wounds
Eternal life now flows.

O Jesus Christ, who sees the love You show,
Which draws You down to pain, distress and woe?
O love Him, then, my brothers,
Love Him above all others!

His all-embracing love draws all men home,
His love surpasses all
And will my heart enthrall.

W.J. 90

THE BEAUTY OF HIS SUFFERING

Scripture reading: Luke 23:46–48

Love is strong as death, jealousy is cruel as the grave. Its flashes are flashes of fire, a most vehement flame. Many waters cannot quench love, neither can floods drown it.

Song of Solomon: 8:6, 7

What made Jesus' suffering so beautiful that people choose to sing of it so often? The events were so dreadful that one would expect everybody to wish to remain silent about them. What makes the passion so attractive? Love! Love radiates from the suffering countenance of Jesus. Love is heard in the gasping, dying words He spoke on the cross. Love shines from His eyes as He beholds the disciple who denied Him. Love envelops the crucified Lord whose body was committed to silent suffering. The two thieves hung on their crosses at either side of Him. Their faces and limbs were probably distorted as they have been portrayed by many Old Masters. How great Jesus' love must have been! Such unimaginable depths of suffering could not extinguish His love. On the contrary, it broke through all suffering in such an overwhelming manner that it became visible to all!

"In suffering there is no deception" is a saying. Suffering reveals the true self. In Jesus' case it was love that shone

125

forth in a purity, depth, beauty and strength beyond imagining. On the cross Jesus redeemed us to enable us to love like this, for it is written that we are "predestined to be conformed to the image of his Son." (Romans 8:29). Who has been redeemed by His love and can now reflect His image?

Come, O sinners, weep, lamenting,
You a cross have dared to raise.
Sun, moon, stars, bow down, cease shining,
Mourn with us and hide your rays,
For the Life and Light of heaven
Now has entered death's dark night,
Christ has died, betrayed, forsaken,
What an agonizing sight!

Weep, O earth, and start lamenting,
You killed Him who made all things.
Mocking, scorning, God rejecting,
Who can measure such great sins?
Nailed to cross in bitter suffering,
He redeemed our sinful race,
Proved with sacrificial offering
God is mercy, love and grace.

WHAT A WONDERFUL SECRET!

Scripture reading: Matthew 27:54–56

Between the throne and the four living creatures and among the elders, I saw a Lamb standing, as though it had been slain.

Revelation 5:6

Jesus on the cross shows us the essence of love. Now, everywhere Love takes people captive. Love has begun His march of victory through the world. The tortured Lamb did not strike back when He was struck. Crucified Love did not make threats when He suffered. He only loved, loved, loved. This is a picture of such power, of such radiant energy and beauty that it shines right down into hell. There, even the captives of death take notice of it. This is the vision that is ceaselessly praised in heaven.

What a wonderful secret! The cross gives birth to salvation and bliss! Suffering gives birth to joy! Nothing on earth has ever released such a stream of bliss as Jesus' suffering and death. Countless people have knelt at the cross of Calvary receiving pardon for their sins and being regenerated. Then as children of God, they have burst forth in a song of rejoicing. O the heights and depths of such a joy! It cannot be compared with any other of this world's joys. Jesus' cross is indeed the source of indescribable joy. Out of suffering flows salvation for many, bringing them bliss and redemption.

Cross of glory, cross of grace,
Carries love to every place,
Tells all men, "God loves you."
Sinners pardon now receive,
If they in the Son believe,
For He has redeemed them.

THE EMPTIED CUP

Scripture reading: John 19:18–22

But we see Jesus, who for a little while was made lower than the angels, crowned with glory and honour because of the suffering of death, so that by the grace of God he might taste death for every one. For it was fitting that he, for whom and by whom all things exist, in bringing many sons to glory, should make the pioneer of their salvation perfect through suffering.

Hebrews 2:9, 10

Jesus hung on the cross. The end of His earthly journey, the final stage of His passion, had been reached. Jesus had to experience again the special sufferings of each of the other stations of the cross, but all together. The God-forsakenness, which probably came to Him for the first time in Gethsemane, now reached its climax on the cross. The suffering of the arrest continued on till He became a captive of death on the cross. He was not only bound to the cross, but nailed on to it to die. The suffering of the crown of thorns and the mockery were still there. They brought Him double torment. His head was still bowed low beneath the crown of thorns. The scornful cries had pursued Him from the time He was crowned with thorns until the hour of His death. Also the cross which He had carried was still with Him. But now He no longer had to carry it—He hung on it, bloodily nailed to it. Above His head the death sentence could be read so that even the suffering of the trial had followed Him. He had been accused of unlawfully making Himself a king. Therefore He was condemned as "King of the Jews".

All the torments and sufferings that had steadily pursued Jesus now fused in a final assault on Him. Now only one last agony waited to seize Him—death. The full measure of His suffering had to come upon Him at once so that the redemption of His love would be complete. The cup of suffering had to be drained. Jesus' passion on the cross comprised all suffering and powerfully proclaims: Love is invincible. It is the strongest power on earth. It is greater than everything else. It is greater than all types of suffering. Not even death on the cross could kill it. Because Jesus is Love, the resurrection had to follow the crucifixion, for love is immortal. Whoever abides in love abides in God and partakes of eternal life, which is God Himself.

The crucifixion was the climax of all the torture and suffering of the body, soul and Spirit of the Son of God. Hell and His enemies had triumphed—God is dead! But behold! The end is the beginning! Life is born in death! Light dawns from the night! Love triumphantly springs from the clutches of death as the Prince of victory, and begins His triumphant march! The Lion of the tribe of Judah, the Lamb of God, has conquered!

I adore You, O Jesus. You won complete redemption through Your torture and suffering. O Lamb, slain upon the cross, You brought us full salvation.

We worship the heights, the depth and the breadth of such a redemption. It is eternal, perfect and all-embracing. It can free all mankind from the power of Satan, from sin and death.

THE SABBATH OF JESUS' SUFFERING

Now there was a man named Joseph from the Jewish town of Arimathea. He was a member of the council, a good and righteous man, who had not consented to their purpose and deed, and he was looking for the kingdom of God. This man went to Pilate and asked for the body of Jesus. Then he took it down and wrapped it in a linen shroud, and laid him in a rock-hewn tomb, where no one had yet ever been laid. It was the day of Preparation, and the sabbath was beginning. The women who had come with him from Galilee followed, and saw the tomb, and how his body was laid; then they returned and prepared spices and ointments. On the sabbath they rested according to the commandment.

Luke 23:50–56

Jesus, His sufferings ended,
Rests in His Father's love,
The Sabbath brings the Saviour
Back to His home above,
And stills His pain and passion;
The Father's sweet compassion
Will ease His Son in Sabbath calm.

O sweet repose and holy
Upon the Father's breast!
All pain and effort ended
Christ's tortured soul finds rest.
O Sabbath of blest union
Renewing the communion
Of God the Holy Trinity.

O Sabbath peace most holy,
A message from above,
Descending from the Father,
Expressing God's great love.
His Father's arms embrace Him
To staunch His pain and sufferings,
With love and peace to soothe His grief.

THE SECOND SABBATH—OF THE LAMB OF GOD

Scripture reading: Luke 23:50–56

And on the seventh day God finished his work which he had done, and he rested on the seventh day from all his work which he had done. So God blessed the seventh day and hallowed it, because on it God rested from all his work which he had done in creation.

Genesis 2:2, 3

Sabbath! There was a stillness in heaven. But it was quite different from the Sabbath when God rested after the six days of Creation. Now a different work had been completed—the work of redemption.

Sabbath! Rest in heaven, after the hosts of angels had been moved by depths of emotion as never before. They had suffered with their Creator. They had wept and lamented over His agony.

Sabbath! Only those who come from fierce battle and deep grief can appreciate what is contained in this word. But no grief can approach the grief which the Son of God endured, both as Man and God, during the days of the passion. Therefore there could never be a soul who experienced a Sabbath as He did.

Sabbath! A task achieved! But not a joyful work of creation. No, a work of suffering for the Creator. His love inclined itself to lost and degenerate creation to draw it home with love and imprint the Creator's dignity upon it.

Sabbath of suffering—not celebrated at the throne of heaven, but in the sepulchre. But still it was Sabbath! A labour had been completed, with His last drop of energy, with the sacrifice of His life—the task of redeeming the whole world.

Sabbath, Sabbath, day of resting,
Who can understand this song?
Those with grief and suffering wrestling
For this holy Sabbath long.

Paschal sunshine, still far distant,
Beams there, hid from human eyes;
Like the planet in the dawning,
Herald of the glad sun's rise.

Peace, deep peace, that knows no measure
Steals like incense through the tomb,
In its folds all pain forgotten,
Dereliction's dread and gloom.

And this Sabbath peace holds promise
Of the resurrection day,
When the Lord of life victorious
Death's grim reign shall end for aye.

W.J. 80

Lord Jesus,

We worship You. You came from eternity, from the kingdom of peace, and yet You did not grant Yourself any rest. You fought even when it meant shedding blood and went the way of the cross. We worship You. Your path of death ended with the Sabbath of redemption. Let us not shy away from battle, the cross and suffering, so that we too may enter the peace of the Sabbath after a hard fight. Let us be Your true followers so that we may partake of Your peace. For You grant peace to those who have laid down their lives in the brave fight against Satan, against flesh and blood.

We thank You for leading us and paving the way, so that we can be victorious in the battle and receive a crown. You have paved the way for us to enter Jerusalem, the city of eternal peace. There we will enter into the eternal rest of God, and celebrate the Sabbath without end.

Now ends the passion way at last,
The darkest night of sin has passed,
The Sabbath day will bring Him peace,
The cross's pain and suffering cease.

Though hard the battle, now it's won!
'Twill fruit and glory bring the Son.
He was so hated, scourged and mocked,
But now He enters rest of God.

Now the peace of paradise
Creeps through the place where Jesus lies.
The angels bow, with soft lament,
And fill the grave with heavenly scent.

THE NEW CREATION

Scripture reading: Revelation 5:9–13

And God saw everything that he had made, and behold, it was very good.
And he who sat upon the throne said, "Behold, I make all things new." Also he said, "Write this, for these words are trustworthy and true."

Genesis 1:31; Revelation 21:5

Now the work of redemption achieved through the suffering of God's Son had been completed. Could the Father do anything but say, as He did after the creation, "It was very

135

good"? Jesus, scarred with wounds, was resting from His suffering and strenuous battle. The Father probably turned to Him and said over and over again, "My Son, it is all good, very good." Yes, He had redeemed *all*, He had set everything right. He had not only restored the old creation, He had created paradise, which far surpassed the old creation: the city of God, springing from the blood of the wounds, where the five wounds of the Lamb shine forth (Revelation 21:23).

What a glorious creation, purposefully renewed through the shedding of God's blood! In amazing radiance this creation shines forth as the reward for the bitter suffering. But the Lamb, our God, who bears the wounds, surpasses the whole creation of heaven and earth. His disciples who have followed Him along the way of suffering, will shine forth with Him in heavenly glory like the sun in their Father's kingdom.

My Saviour Christ now finds repose,
His weary eyelids calmly close;
The hostile clamour round Him dies,
In linen soft He silent lies.

My Saviour's suffering now is done,
He bowed His head, the victory won;
Now rests He in the silent cave
Where they have laid Him in His grave.

Let all now leave Him here to rest,
Anoint and bind those wounds so blest;
And kneeling there with downcast eyes,
Await the day that He shall rise.

Bewail His wounds with sorrow deep,
His bitter death bemoan and weep;
Let penitential tears now fall,
Most precious salve and balm of all.

In Father's arms He lies at last,
Soon He'll go home, His torture past,
And His deep wounds will then be healed
With Father's kiss, His grief consoled.

W.J. 78

THE THIRD SABBATH—OF THE WORLD

Scripture reading: 1 Corinthians 15:22–28

And I heard a great voice from the throne saying, "Behold, the dwelling of God is with men. He will dwell with them, and they shall be his people, and God himself will be with them; he will wipe away every tear from their eyes, and death shall be no more, ... for the former things have passed away."

Revelation 21:3, 4

Now the Sabbath of the world has to come! Now the Sabbath of suffering is over and the Holy Trinity looks for the great day of the world's Sabbath. The perfection of the world will come. All will be united and return to the heart of the Godhead. (1 Corinthians 15: 28).Then everything will be bathed in Sabbath peace. Yes, God is waiting for this Sabbath when the whole universe, His creation, will reflect His glory and true beauty. Men will be redeemed and happy. They will bear the features of God.

Heaven will come down to earth and the dwelling of God will be with men. He will live among them.

The Sabbath calls to us, "God is seeking helpers so that the day of peace for the world may soon come." All the bells of heaven will ring on that day, because creation will have returned home to its Creator.

He who loves Jesus will not rest until the kingdom of his Saviour, the Bridegroom, is established. Jesus has purchased it with such torture—it must come. Jesus' blood was shed in such agony that whoever loves Him will suffer with Him until this blood has accomplished its purpose in creation. Those who love Him will be willing to share in the fellowship of His suffering, in order to help Him carry out His work of perfecting the world.

The Sabbath of His love and suffering will become the Sabbath of the world—of the perfecting of the world. This will be the perfect victory of love. The foundation for the perfecting of mankind and of the universe was laid in Jesus' sacrificial death. Therefore it will truly come.

Lord, let Your Sabbath come for all, the Sabbath of the world and the nations, the Sabbath of the last day. Then, O God, You will be all in all. The dwelling of God will be with men and the earth will become paradise. You, the holy Creator and Redeemer, will be able to celebrate the Sabbath of the world, because all enemies will have been laid at the feet of Your Son. Men will have returned home to Your fatherly heart.

Sabbath! O earth, rejoice!
Praise God with heart and voice,
For the last foe is o'ercome.
Throned on earth, God now reigns,
Ever with men remains,
Love has accomplished all this.

Sabbath joy fills God's heart,
All sorrow must depart,
Salvation now is fulfilled.
All worship Him with love,
Can never praise enough
The Lord who brought them all home.

W.J.167

EPILOGUE

SUFFERING BRINGS GLORY

There is an empty tomb at the end of Jesus' way of passion Death has been changed into resurrection and eternal life. What has come out of His way of suffering and death? Victory and resurrection, joy and exultation! This truly is the Easter message. It shows us the end of all ways of suffering. It tells us that the path of the passion and Good Friday were not the end in our Lord Jesus' life. No, Good Friday was followed by Easter. Out of death, life broke forth. It is equally true that suffering will never be the end for us either. Jesus' sorrow and tears were transformed into joy. This will happen in our lives also.

Jesus trod the path of the passion because of our sin. He chose death and the grave in order to redeem us. If we go the way of death with Jesus, the old Adam of our sin will slowly and surely die. Then the new Adam, created in God's image, will arise. How wonderful! A critical, hard, unmerciful soul becomes filled with love and goodness. A dominating, self-willed soul begins to show gentleness. Pride is transformed into humility. This is indeed one of God's wonders. A change takes place in us when we commit our ego to a way of constant dying. God made the gift of Easter to His beloved Son. He will also make a gift of Easter to everyone who follows Jesus along His way of the cross. Easter assures us that no single soul, nor group of people can remain in death when they willingly follow paths of suffering with Jesus and ever anew say, "Yes Father", and submit to the death of their ego. But the resurrection applies only to people who are bound to Jesus, the Prince of life, and go His way. For those who choose to go the way of bitterness and hatred and who will not let the ego die, there can be no life out of death.

So dying is the secret of the Easter victory. Powers that previously had influence over us can no longer use this influence when we have gone the way of the dying grain of wheat. In our life the power of the enemy will be broken in so far as we follow our Lord on His way of the cross, steadfastly trusting in His victory. The powers of death and hell were vanquished when Jesus was completely delivered up to them, because He continued to love and endure like a lamb. Therefore the chains of death were burst asunder and He rose from the grave. The enemy could no longer hold anything against Him—the guards lay on the ground as though dead.

This is also the way to resurrection for us. Only those who go the way of death with Jesus and fall into the ground, like grains of wheat, will win the joy and glory of the Easter victory in their personal lives. If we go the way of death, with faith in Jesus' victorious resurrection, we will experience a joyful resurrection in this life, and will one day possess eternal life in heavenly glory.

Other Books by Basilea Schlink Which You May Wish to Read:

When God Calls—$1.25
The intriguing autobiography of Basilea Schlink, tracing her spiritual adventures to the founding of the Sisterhood.
Original title: *Er Zeigt Der Wege Sinn*, 1968. Foreign translations: Swedish, 1969; Norwegian, 1969; English, 1970-71; Danish, 1971; Finnish, 1971; Dutch, 1972; Hebrew, 1972; Indonesian, 1972.

My All for Him—$1.25
A moving collection of powerful meditations on the demands of God upon Christians, and the happiness which follows obedience.
Original title: *Alles Fuer Einen*, 1969. Foreign translations: Norwegian, 1970; Indonesian, 1970; English, 1971-72; Italian, 1973.

You Will Never Be the Same—$1.45
A highly illuminating series of short chapters describing how to successfully deal with specific sins still clinging to the Christian's life.
Original title: *So Wird Man Anders*, 1971. Foreign translations: English, 1972; Norwegian, 1972; Swedish, 1972; Dutch, 1973; Finnish, 1973.

Hope for Man in a Hopeless World—95¢
An appraisal of the causes of the world's present plight, and a declaration of the "way out" by cooperation with God.
Original title: *Und Keiner Wollte Es Glauben*, 1964. Foreign translations: Danish, 1965; Dutch, 1965; Swedish, 1966; French, 1966; English, 1967-72; Finnish, 1967.

Ruled by the Spirit—$1.25
The power of God available today to dedicated Christians. Plus testimonies from among the Sisterhood which indicate how an invigorating working relationship with the Holy Spirit may be enjoyed.
Original title: *Wo Der Geist Weht*, 1967. Foreign translations: French, 1968; Swedish, 1968; Norwegian, 1968; English, 1970; Dutch, 1970.

Father of Comfort—$1.25
Short devotions for each day of the year, intended to teach how to trust God as Father.
Original title: *Der Niemand Traurig Sehen Kann*, 1965. Foreign translations: Greek, 1968; French,

1970; Indonesian, 1970; Italian, 1971; English, 1971-72; Arabic, 1972; Chinese (Mand.), 1972; Norwegian, 1972.

Behold His Love—$1.45
This book is addressed to those who desire to meditate prayerfully on the passion of Jesus, so that they may be led more and more into the way of the cross and into the unity of love with those who love Him.

A Matter of Life and Death—95¢
The rape of planet earth—what caused it, and what to do to remedy it. Carefully documented treatment of the widely discussed problem of global pollution.
Original title: *Umweltverschmutzung Und Dennoch Hoffnung*, 1972. Foreign translations: Dutch, 1973; Finnish, 1973; Italian, 1973; Swedish, 1973.

World in Revolt (booklet)—25¢
An astute review and analysis of the waves of revolution rolling over the modern world, and a plain statement on what can be done about it.

Praying Our Way Through Life (booklet)—25¢
Counsel on how to react to God during suffering, times of unanswered prayer, temptations, worry, despondency, and fear.
Original title: *Mein Beten*, 1969. Foreign translations: English, 1970-71; Swedish, 1971; Norwegian, 1971; Chinese (Mand.), 1971; Indonesian, 1972; Finnish, 1972; Arabic, 1973.

Never Before in the History of the Church (booklet)—50¢
A startling examination of "the Harlot Church" as it exists today in the world.

Mirror of Conscience (booklet)—25¢
A guidebook to earnest Christians genuinely interested in examining the areas of their lives in which they may need victory.

It Shall Come To Pass (booklet)—25¢
A delightfully sympathetic consideration of the attitude older Christians should have toward the "Jesus People."

Available at your local Christian bookstore, or BETHANY FELLOWSHIP, INC., 6820 Auto Club Rd., Minneapolis, Minnesota 55438.